TRUST

WITHOUT

BORDERS

Courage Like No Other

To Karen &
Tom

I. Ariel Maskil

Trilogy Christian Publishers
A Wholly Owned Subsidiary of Trinity Broadcasting Network
2442 Michelle Drive
Tustin, CA 92780

For information, address Trilogy Christian Publishing
Rights Department, 2442 Michelle Drive, Tustin, Ca 92780.
Trilogy Christian Publishing/ TBN and colophon are trademarks of Trinity Broadcasting Network.

For information about special discounts for bulk purchases, please contact Trilogy Christian Publishing.

Manufactured in the United States of America

10 9 8 7 6 5 4 3 2 1

Library of Congress Cataloging-in-Publication Data is available.

ISBN 978-1-64773-841-9 (Print Book)
ISBN 978-1-64773-842-6 (ebook)

CONTENTS

ACKNOWLEDGMENT

I must confess that the major contents of this book have not been conceived by me. This book is a result from a series of dreams commencing in May 2016 through January 2020. The revelations and significant details have been completely downloaded and transcribed from these dreams. My only major contribution toward this endeavor has been to act as a scribe and to add names to each character in the book. This was not done lightly. My inclusion of their names in this book was based upon how I believe that they would have conducted themselves and how they would have responded to the call to respond to God's request or the call to LOT (listen, obey, and trust).

I wish to thank my wife, Jeanne, and my daughter, Michelle, for their assistance in reading, commenting, and correcting several grammatical errors for the first draft. I also wish to thank approximately seven other individuals, especially Joe Crème, Steve Bodi, and Steven Banasik, who took the time to read the draft script and offer insight on the content. For the record, there were no significant content changes other than toning down some of the verbiage.

I wish to immensely thank the proofreaders, editors, publisher, and several others behind the scenes from Trilogy Publishing and TBN Television for all their assistance since this was the first time I have been involved in a book. The Lord calls not the qualified, but qualifies those He calls and He makes a way for those who obey His call.

It was the spring of 2027, with the trees in full bloom. Winter had come early and seemed to have ended by the first week of March. April showers also came early. The midafternoon mist was refreshing and cleared the pollen from the air.

We lived in a small town named Bethel, which had approximately twenty-six hundred permanent residents situated in the central portion of the state just ten miles north of the lake region in a mountain valley just off the old north–south country road mainly utilized by area locals. The initial settlers in the town were French Canadian trappers. The name of the founding family clan was Luz, and the hamlet was initially called Luz but later became a small village, and then they called the town Luzdale. It was just a little hamlet for most of the 1700s through the mid-1800s. Then in the late 1800s, a group of Jewish entrepreneurs from Rhode Island, New York, and Massachusetts moved in. They purchased most of the area north of the mountains and soon renamed the town Bethel. They called it that because the mountains formed a Gilgal as Jacob would worship God as well as his experiencing God in a place called Bethel, meaning "house of God." The north side of the mountains looked like a stairway, as identified in "Jacob's ladder," while the south side was very steep and very difficult, if not impossible, to traverse in most of the areas.

They built textile plants, barrel manufacturing companies, and later, a ball bearing manufacturing facility. They sponsored more French Canadians to come to the village to work in the mills and plants. The mill and plant owners built a Jewish temple for themselves in the northern area of the village, and a Catholic church for the workers in the southern area near the mountain pass. They owned the general stores, a bank, meeting halls, the local railroads, the black-smith facilities, and stagecoach companies. East of Bethel was a little town named Hai, which was located on the east side of the mountain range. It was impossible to get there from Bethel, but one had to go completely around the mountain range. The Frenchman owned the saloons and construction companies.

Later, summer homes were built in the neighboring area seven miles south of the pass in the lake region, and they called it Zoar. This village of about 420 people in the 1950s grew to a population of over 35,000. In the 1960s, a couple of thousand hippies and free-love types moved into the village. The bar scene became the thing, and several nude beaches sprung up all over at the area lakes, which attracted another, more-perverted crowd. Throughout the seventies, the village kept expanding and nude bars, houses of the rising sun, popped up all over the village, attracting others to settle in. By the late 1980s, the town had grown to over 20,000 and had become a tourist attraction of perversion with solar festivals every June 21.

In the 1990s, the gay rights movement added a new dimension of perversion when a state court ordered the town to allow the gays to enter floats in their summer parade. Soon gay bars and sex parlors appeared, and the town grew to over thirty thousand by 2010. Before 2020, the mayor, chief of police, and four of the five councilmen were either gay or transvestites. Last count, the village had over thirty-five thousand people with sex, nudity, drunkards, drugs sold everywhere, and many other houses of perversion springing up weekly. Crimes of perversions always remained unsolved and were ignored by the police, who rarely investigated. Zoar had become the modern-day Sodom, or sin city. Over the past seven years, the regulars moved out and weirder things started to happen when satanist started to arrive.

In the early 1900s, a group of Methodists moved into Bethel, just north of the lake, and built a church. They loved the lake area and built a hotel and resort areas for tourists. They promoted water sports, camping, and boating in the summer, and skiing in the win-ter. They also built conference centers for businessmen's getaway and executive resorts. The trains were still running up until the mid-

1950s, and motorcars became fashionable after that, so roads were built in the late 1950s and early 1960s over the old railroad tracks from the south of the village.

The village grew to approximately seven thousand through the early 1940s, but after the mills and the plants started to shut down in the early 1950s, most of the people left to find employment elsewhere. As the mills and plants started to shut down, the owners sold off the real estate. One of the barrels and ball-bearing manufacturing plants was the last to shut down in the mid-1990s.

When the mills closed, many of the older, wealthier Jews moved away to Florida or New York while the younger men moved to Israel. Only a few dozen remained in the town after the closings. They had enough wealth to sustain themselves, while some still owned the bank, a few stores, while the others were lawyers or professionals in the village. They were well respected and very generous to the community. They paid for the construction of the local high school and the beautiful park in the 1920s. In the late 1950s, they paid for the construction of the main street as it exists today. They constructed a beautiful, well-treed avenue with plenty of parking for the stores and shops lining the way for their synagogue at the north end of town to the town hall in the southern portion of the town.

The new main interstate highway was constructed in the 1990s thirty miles east on the other side of the mountains' principal north–south route to the tourist vacation areas in the central and northern regions.

Bethel was nestled between two sets of mountain ranges, with a lake on the northern side of the east mountain and a swamp, conservation area, and animal sanctuary on the southern side of the west mountain. The southern lake region was about fifteen miles to the south.

The mountain height varied from a thousand feet to the east to over fourteen hundred feet to the west, but because of the ravine, it looked like over two thousand feet from the base of the ravine. The mountains almost formed a funnel in the south. The mountain pass and the access road were about 4,500 feet long from the northerly mouth of the pass to the second bend in the road as one headed south. The first bend on in the road was approximately 1,200 feet from the southerly entrance to the pass, which followed the contour of the mountain on the east.

The mountain on the west-side slope ranged from about 1,000 feet to approximately 1,400 feet, where there was the great cavern, which went for miles along a river flowing south at the base of the cavern and down toward the lake region. The cavern is over seven hundred feet deep from the road to the river. Just west of there were the wild-life sanctuary and the swamp located at the base of the west mountain.

As we drove up from the south heading toward Bethel, we'd have to follow the road carved in the side of the mountain, which was paved over the old, abandoned railroad track. The ravine was on the right, and the mountains on the left range, from a few hundred feet to over a thousand feet.

As we drove north from Zoar, there were several bends in the road, with the mountain ledges on the right and the ravine on the left. After crossing the bridge over the river, we approached the series of bends in the road with the ravine on the left.

As we rounded the first bend traveling north from Zoar, and after crossing the bridge, we started seeing high walls of the mountain on the right. The railroad company in the mid-1800s had carved out the road to the south of the eastern mountain slope to lay the tracks and carved the hundred-or-so-foot-wide mountain pass adjacent to the seven-hundred-foot cavern or ravine below, next to where the eastern mountain range met the western mountain slope.

After passing the first bend, we started heading toward the second bend, where the ravine commenced to increase in depth.

After passing the second bend, we headed toward the third bend from Zoar, or the first bend from the pass carved through the mountains. The ravine's depth increased to over seven hundred feet. As we approached the first bend, we could see a steep drop-off.

Once we passed the bend, we traveled approximately 1,200 feet to the pass. The pass between the two mountains ran approximately a thousand feet.

As we looked from the south from a mountain just north of the town toward the mountain pass, we could see beautiful forest and the main road leading to the larger town with a population of just over thirty-five thousand. The plush green forest and great mountain scenery was always spectacular in the fall and in the spring.

The mayor and the counsel had signs posted in the swamp area warning people to stay out of the swamp because about twenty years ago, a tourist disposed of their pet fish into the swamp and we found out that the fish were piranhas.

In that same year, another tourist released two venomous snakes near the same swamp in the marsh and conservation area. The area was also full of hornets and other bees, so most of the villagers stayed away from this area anyway.

At the northerly face of the mountain pass, George and Moe built themselves mountain homes carved into the mountain. George's home was built into the easterly mountain and contained nearly six thousand square feet of living space and two thousand square feet of storage plus the garage space. It was set up in multi-levels, and the entrance of his home was through the garage built with twelve-inch concrete, with a face covered by the rocks all around it. It blended in with the mountain and was hardly noticeable. As we looked from the church grounds, we could barely see their homes.

George always said that he was prepared for anything. His home was self-sufficient, with multiple fuel-source generator, a cistern capable of holding over five thousand gallons of water, metal-reinforced window shutters, and many other extras. George was able to tap into a spring of water and divert it into his cistern, and the overflow would run through his living space, which acted like a coolant for the unit. During the winter, he could divert the water away from the living area and have the water drain down the mountain. He had several inside stairways and an elevator going from the lower level, where the garage was located, to the fourth-most upper level, where his family and entertainment room was located. The home was also set up with solar power, with the panels on the northern slope, facing east and west.

He had security cameras located at all angles and views, which was very picturesque at sunrise and sunset. The security cameras were wired into his computer and multiple television sets, which were throughout the house. His kitchen was at the fourth level, along with a large dining room and family room. His bedrooms were in the third level, with a large entertainment area and bar. His upper level was a large entertain area he used during the summer.

The second level was storage, which was adjacent and above the garage, and George claimed he had two years' supply of food stored in one of the areas. George's lowest level was where the garage was located, and it was built like a German war bunker. The entrance of the garage was up the mountain, about fifty feet above the roadway, with a dirt driveway winding for more than 350 feet long to the entrance of the garage. Each level of the unit was carved into the granite mountain and contained more than 1,200 square feet at each level.

There were four entrances to the upper levels onto patios facing the south, north, and west, and each entrance was secured with double steel doors. One of the exits led to a twelve- to fifteen-foot-wide path alongside the mountain, which would take you to an overlook point at the first bend in the road south of the pass. The exit on the second level was forty-five feet above the pass, while the fourth-level exit was ninety feet above the roadway of the pass. The fifth level was twenty feet higher.

The mountain pass carved out by the railroad company looked like three large steps each about forty to forty-five feet high between the steps. George's mountain path could reach both the second and the third levels of these paths of this easterly mountain.

Moe and Irene's home were built into the western mountainside of the pass. Although not as elaborate as George's home, it was about forty-nine hundred square feet of living space and eighteen hundred square feet of storage space, including a two-car garage. They also had a multilevel home with an elevator built into the west side of the home. Each floor had approximately a thousand square feet, with large granite stairways going to each level. The upper fifth level was an entertainment and living area that opened onto a very large patio facing the south and the east, which also wrapped around to the north from the east and the west. The upper fourth level was where the kitchen was located with a large dining area off in the kitchen, which also opened to a patio on the east side and a large courtyard on the south side. The second level had their living room, study, Irene's office, and "prayer closet." The patio that led from the north- to the south-side courtyard was around twenty-five feet in width.

The third level contained three large bedrooms, Moe's office, and a study. The lower level was where the storage areas were located, which was above the garage. Their driveway was five hundred feet long, which was paved and wound around the north face of the mountain. Moe had a swimming pool built into the granite mountain that was fed by an inner mountain stream. The pool was off the upper level, built into the east side of the west mountain at the fourth level. Moe and Irene had great views from the southern and northern sides of their home.

Brendan Lynch

George, Moe, and Irene had been friends for more than fifty years. When Moe was going to high school and college, he worked for George at his gas station. Both George and Moe sold their businesses in another state and moved to this quiet village when they were in their mid-seventies.

Bethel had a beautiful park just off the center of Main Street. The town built its recreation field adjacent to the park. In the center of the park was a large platform for summer concerts and for school graduations. The platform was enclosed on three sides, and it was in the shape of an octagon.

There were loudspeakers all through the park and the Main Street boulevard, so everyone could hear the concerts. Every Fourth of July, there would be a concert with fireworks displays between the lake and the park. Vendors would set up tents to sell their fireworks and other products on the village green near the park.

The lake and its beaches were located between the park and the eastern mountain range. Off to the northwest of the lake was another beautiful park with several recreation areas for baseball, football/soccer, basketball, and tennis, and it even had an outdoor skating area for boarding and rollerblading for the youngsters.

Throughout and between the two parks were many benches, grilling areas, and picnic tables, as well as camping areas with restrooms and water faucets. The fields, the lake, and the mountain views were spectacular. During the summer, campers could erect tents in the northern area of the park and areas northwest of the lake.

On the north side of the lake were condominium developments that sold time-share units and contained over six hundred units and functioned as hotels during the summer and winter seasons. The development was built thirty years ago, and many of the original buyers no longer owned their unit weeks. The developers picked up all the defaulted unit time slots over the past fifteen years, and the facilities now mainly operated as hotels. They were a truly well-operated and well-maintained facility, and the managers were town residents. It had a great view of the lake and the mountains on the east and south.

When we looked to the west of the town, we saw a spectacular view of the mountains to the west of the town. There were many fields and undeveloped land around the town. The flowers of the fields were some beautiful in the springtime, and the farmers used the pastures in the summer and fall to graze their cows and horses. The farmers sold their milk, fruits, and vegetables at the local downtown stores and along the roadways when tourists came. They offered tours of the farms, horseback-riding sessions, and some even had bed-and-breakfast facilities.

The west-side mountains behind the wood of the church gradually sloped to the peaks but then had a major drop on the west face for over a thousand feet to the swift river below.

The layout of the town was very orderly, with the stores and commercial areas lining up from the town hall at one end and the old synagogue at the other end of a beautifully maple-treed avenue.

The synagogue was later converted into a community center for the kids. There were plenty of parking from the street, with two one-way lanes running north to south or south to north. The parking areas were in front of the shops, as well as selected areas between the two lanes. There was another service road in the rear of the shops for trucks to unload their merchandise, which freed up the boulevard for the shoppers.

It was a quaint little town that looked like it was built in the late 1940s, just after the Great War. It had one movie house, one pharmacy, a clinic, a large grocery store, two convenience stores with gas stations, a hardware store, a few clothing stores, a bank, a credit union, two barbershops and three hair salons, five restaurants, six pubs, an Army-Navy shop, a few specialty shops, and a few other miscellaneous types of stores.

On the outskirts of town, there were a construction company, building supply store, lumber yard, storage yard, quarry, junkyard, our church (although there had been three previously). The closed plants and mills were located at the northern side of outskirts of the town.

The town was composed of a variety of different ethnic backgrounds, with French and English Canadian roots constituting the largest groups. We had a dentist, two lawyers, three accountants, two doctors, one mortgage broker, a financial advisor, one Catholic priest, two Protestant ministers, a rabbi, an Amman, three engineering firms, two electricians, two plumbers, an HVAC firm, and several other various types of construction- and equipment-related companies. We had several other tradesmen who worked in the neighboring towns within forty miles.

The larger Catholic church to the south of the town had two camps, which had been formerly used by the Boy and Girl Scouts for summer Bible camp and for retreats each summer. The camp had both cabins and tents, which could house nearly two hundred campers. The cabins were now being used by the church to house the homeless vets.

The new mayor and several leading town residents were not too happy the church was doing this. They wanted the church to make them move out of town and go somewhere else. They even told the church to stop feeding them so they could move on. The new mayor said, "Just like a stray cat, if you feed it, it will stay, but if you don't feed it, it will go away." The church decided to appoint the homeless as camp directors and maintenance personnel, which allowed them to watch over the grounds and stay in the cabins.

The old-timers gathered on the park benches, reminiscing of the days gone by and marveling at how things had changed since their childhood. Remembering the decades of their youth from the late 1950s, 1960s, and early 1970s. They even talked about the days gone by when their parents fought for our country in World War II and the Korean War. The graduating classes of the late 1960s through the 1970s fostered the "Hell no, we won't go!" slogan during the mid-Vietnam War era. All of them had parents who stood up for their country, uncles who made the ultimate sacrifice so that freedom and democracy would continue to ring not only in America but also in foreign lands.

The fight against communism and oppression became an obsession, which became misdirected and misinterpreted by the world and even by those at home. As America pressed its agenda, so did the hidden governments of the world's elite continue to maneuver their agenda for a one-world government. They strived for a reduction of the population and for the re-establishment of an autocratic society of past centuries with them in control. They controlled much of the world's wealth and key industries, which enabled them to thrive in the bad times as well as in the good time.

Their generation was born out of the baby boomers of the mid-1940s to the 1950s. They were the generation of fast cars and wild times. They held on to their parents' Judeo-Christian beliefs through their teenage years and twenties. It seemed that life and the world changed in the mid-sixties, when many of them graduated from high school. The principals of the high schools where many of them graduated told their class that the class was the beginning of the down-fall of Western civilization. They often said their generation was an unruly, immoral bunch of drunks. They even canceled their class trips in retaliation for the previous class trip's antics and their overall class's poor conduct.

Many times, their senior class officers all came from wealthy families, and most of them even had their own apartments while in their senior years of high school, which enabled a constant "party time" on the weekends. They were the "golden spoon" kids of that generation. Our personal groups of friends were not part of the elite crowd because we came from the poor and the working class. I was the only Jewish boy in a Catholic high school. There were about a dozen Protestants at the school, but 98 percent of the school were Catholic, taught by religious brothers and priests from Canada.

As we walked through the park, I saw Moe, Irene, Michelle, Gary, Rick, Diane, Forshia, Eric, Josh, and Hailey cooking on the grill. His brother Roger was with them. Also with them were Tom and his wife, Monique. Monique and Michelle were the daughters of Irene and Moe. Moe's real name was Maurice, but when his girls were young, they thought that he was named after a cat, Morris, because of the commercials.

Moe's father had been a career Navy man, and his brother Roger joined the Navy as soon as he graduated from high school. They called Roger, Spider because he could do the "limbo dance" the best, in which he was less than a quarter-inch from the floor. No one could beat him in the competition. All the girls loved him, and he tried to love all the girls. Captain Roger also served eight years in the Air Force and sixteen years as a pilot in the Army. He served three two-year tours of duty during the Vietnam War. He became messed up physically because of the Agent Orange effect. He had had several strokes and was crippled on the right side due to the strokes.

Near them at the next grill was a group of former Vietnam veterans, and they included Jack, Colonel John, Lou, Jim, Henry, Normand, Larry, Mike, Pierre, Joe, Rene, and his wife, Fran. Many of them were homeless prior to coming to the village.

In the late 1960s and into the 1970s, the Vietnam war escalated, and the new draft was instituted. Many went on to either college or junior college to avoid the draft. Others joined the National Guard or Coast Guard to avoid the draft, but the National Guard units were activated, and the Coast Guard was called up to patrol the waterways of Vietnam. We all lost friends during that war. The war was looked upon as a total failure by the general public in the 1970s, and the men coming back from the war were mistreated by the liberal radicals and they belittled them, calling them "baby killers" or "potheads."

The military was hampered by the opinions of the liberal media, teachers, and professors in our schools and colleges who never served their country but only served their own self-image. They believed in total freedom but not fighting for that freedom. They believed freedom can be negotiated because all people want the same things. They believed that communism was another acceptable form of government and that wealth should be shared by all and not necessarily earned. They neglected to look at the facts that communism was just a tool of another group controlling the masses under a utopian theory that was not workable. They did not realize wealth without work and achievement without effort is not attainable in the long run. Everyone becomes equal when everyone is poor, but then the powerful will overtake them and rule over them.

Many of the returning vets were shunned by their liberal peers. War had taken its toll on the men who saw many of their buddies killed in the firefights with the Cong. The scars of death permeated their very souls, and their anger affected their moral fortitude to a numbing point that the kill-or-be-killed mentality took over their judgment. If a man had a gun, he must be an enemy and must be killed. If a person was from the Far East, you could not tell whether he was a friend or a foe, so one could not take any chances with them.

Our church knew that one's life experiences or troubles could make one either better or bitter. If we learn from our experiences, we become better, but if we live or dwell in the past, we will become bitter. We must live in the consequences of our or of others' stupidities

26

and attitudes. Giving up on life is not an option; we cannot quit or give in to the misdirected statements or actions of others.

As we continued to walk through the park, I noted numerous other retired individuals. Most were members of our church. For the past ten years, we all were on a first-name basis, and now I even forgot most of their last names. Our church members were ridiculed daily by most youngsters and post-millennials, who were the children of the liberal parents. They called us many demeaning names, such as "the church of the ancients," because the average age of our members was in the upper seventies. The generation under forty years old looked upon religious beliefs as old-school and useless. They said believing in a god was just a crutch for weak-minded old people who were going to die soon.

Even some of the church leaders in other nearby communities made erroneous statements, like, "There are many ways to heaven!" The Bible prophecy did state, as it is written, "Even the elect shall be deceived." This added to the confusion of the nonbelievers. Our church was a true Bible-based teaching congregation.

We were the remnants of the church. Despite the profession of faith by their grandparents, the majority of the next three generations drifted away from believing that God does exist and that He truly loves us. They listened to their unbelieving friends, teachers, and professors, who claimed that there is no God and that religion is the opium of the masses, just as Karl Mark had preached over a hundred years earlier, claiming that a god was just a fabrication of the imagination to control people's beliefs or to make money from. In the past forty years, the media, the government, and the perverts eroded the belief in God in the name of total freedom, equality, liberalism, progressiveness, and self-fulfillment. This was a method to promote their form of communism or their personal lifestyle.

We reached a point in our society that the Isaiah 5:20 prophecy was being revealed before our very eyes: "Woe to those who call evil good, and good evil; who put darkness for light and light for darkness; who up bitter for sweet, and sweet for bitter." Our society changed greatly during our lifetime, where one masked their perversion in the name of freedom and free choice was the moral code.

God's laws and God's standards were considered ancient, and even the elect was being deceived in the name of God by relaxing the standards God set for civilization. The Ten Commandments became the "ten suggestions." The government passed laws by allowing abortions up to one hour after birth should the mother not desire to retain the child or should the child have some deformity.

The mothers sacrificed their newborns to Baal, the god idol. Their Baal idol was their career, their shame, their mistake, their promiscuity, or what others would think. The last item was becoming a farce. Women became more involved in "women's rights and empowerment," and children became a burden during their period of upward mobility. The movement was fine at first but soon became more like women dominance than women equality. Many sorted powers over men, and even over other lesser women.

The jezebel spirit spread across America during the Obama years, pushing false ideologies and creating multiple divisions among the population, which continued to divide groups of beliefs so that control could be exercised over the population. The divide-and-conquer methodology. False doctrine and beliefs, as well as false freedoms and rights, continued to make its ways in the hearts and minds of our younger generations, thus confusing them to believe whatever they needed to believe to justify their own personal actions and desires.

The spirit of witchcraft spread into the schools and colleges, with required readings of books like Harry Potter and games like Dungeons and Dragons. The television programs increased programming of the zombies, the walking dead, vampires, and good witches. Sexual immorality and people living together without marriage were glamorized, and fornication and like-kind sexual relationships were touted as being the norm of society and that it was okay. The increase in transgenders reached epic proportions, with six- and eight-year-olds desiring to change their sex like they changed their coats. Of course, these parents expected the insurance companies or government should pay for these operations or changes.

Our church had approximately 150 active members, with most of us being retired. We gathered two and sometimes three times a week, once for service and once for Bible study. We had other meetings for each of the various types of ministries and how the various groups had to minister to the villagers and the homeless.

Our members were active in the community to assist the elderly and the downtrodden. Our church was the only group in town to help the homeless and the poor despite being ridiculed by the other residents and officials of the town. The other residents scolded us by telling us not to feed the homeless so that they did not stay around here, in hope that they'd move on to the next town. We were of the mentality that we had God's love, that there was no grave that was going to hold our body down, neither shame, fear, nor war.

We showed respect and love for those down on their luck. We took care of the homeless and poor by feeding them two meals a day at the church, we clothed them with new or good used clothes, and we provided them with tents and housing paid for by the church and several church members. In the winter, during the extreme cold days, our church community took these poor souls into their homes for days or weeks at a time, and we all shared the burden. We felt that God had blessed us, and we needed to bless the unfortunate in the name of Yehoshua.

On a few occasions, we did not have enough volunteers to house all the homeless, so we took them into the church function rooms when temperatures dropped below zero. The mayor and the other elected officials threatened to take us to court because the church was violating zoning laws for housing more than four unrelated individuals, because we were not zoned as a hotel, B&B, or rooming house. They threatened to fine the church and close us down. One of the members of our church had been the mayor of the town for years, but he lost the election only because he was a member of the church who violated the laws by feeding and housing "undesirables." The new mayor started to persecute the church and its members for caring for these groups. They claimed that our town was a magnet for all "those people" and the town could not afford to support them. Truthfully, the town never paid one red cent to house them, feed them, or clothed them. The new mayor of the town also claimed that since we started to feed them, the crime rate of the town tripled. We had not had any crime in the town for over ten years, and the only crimes he could point to were the violations of the new "panhandling" laws, which the mayor and selectmen passed shortly after the new mayor was elected.

Our church was unique in the fact that, initially, for financial reasons, we combined the local Catholic church, the local Protestant church, and the Jewish synagogue into one facility. None of our individual churches could afford any longer to support each of our individual buildings, so the Protestant church and then the Jewish synagogue decided to sell their buildings and pool the funds to maintain the larger Catholic church, which also had a kitchen and banquet room in the basement, a small school, and several offices and meeting rooms. The Catholic church could hold five hundred individuals.

The land or property had been previously placed into an irrevocable trust by a wealthy person who had owned the land and had built the church, school, and meeting place with the stipulation that if the facility had no longer been used as a church, the property was to be sold and the funds donated to another charity hundreds of miles away. He also left trust funds, but prior pastors had spent them in order to maintain the school system, because they offered free tuition to all parishioners.

At first, the congregation held separate services with the Jewish people under me, Rabbi Maskil, which met on either Friday night or on Saturday mornings. They met in the meeting hall of the school. The Jewish congregation dwindled from fifty members to now only twelve members. Some died, some moved to assisted-living facilities, while others moved away due to the constant taunting and antisemitic slurs by the younger members of the town. I, Rabbi Maskil, became a Messianic Jew and well versed in the Torah and the New Testament. Some also attributed the decline in the Jewish congregation to the rabbi's acknowledgment of Jesus as the Messiah.

The different groups united shortly after getting together over financial issues facing each group. At this ecumenical meeting, it was agreed that each religious leader would prepare a verse from the Bible or Torah and give a ten-minute sermon using the verse. One of the most powerful verses that ended up uniting the groups were two quotes from the Torah and the Bible. At that joint ecumenical service, which was held on Yom Kippur, or the Jewish day of atonement, the Catholics gathered with the Protestant and Jewish communities and agreed to a twenty-five-hour fast together prior to the service with the Catholics at their church on the southern end of town.

The rabbi read a scripture, quoting from Leviticus 17:11, which read, "For the life of the flesh is in the blood, and I have given it to you upon the alter to make atonement for your souls; for it is the blood that makes atonement for the soul." The rabbi gave a sermon on how the blood makes the atonement for our sins to the Lord. He also incorporated how Yahweh provided Moses and the Hebrews manna, or bread, during the forty years in the desert, and due to their evil ways, they needed to atone. God shed the blood of an animal to provide the skins to cover Adam and Eve after they sinned against Him and were cast out of the garden of Eden. The bread gives our bodies life, but the blood gives our souls life and forgiveness of all our sins through repentance and atonement.

Father Jake's sermon's Bible quote came from Hebrews 9:20–22, which stated, "Moses said, 'This is the blood of the covenant which God has commanded you… And according to the law almost all things are purified with the blood, and without shedding of blood there is no remission.'" His sermon also tied in the Genesis part of Adam and Eve, the skin of the animals clothing their nakedness and their being cast out of the garden with the blood of Jesus, the Messiah. His sermon also talked about the need for the confession and repentance of our sins.

Finally, when Pastor Dave stood up, he said, "The Spirit of God is definitely working among the leadership and the community. My Bible quote is from John 6:53–58, 'Then Jesus said to them, most assuredly, I say to you, unless you eat the flesh of the Son of Man and drink His blood, you have no life in you. Whoever eats My flesh and drinks My blood has eternal life, and I will raise him up at the Last day. For My flesh is food indeed and My blood is drink indeed. He who eats My flesh and drinks My blood abides in Me and I in him. As the living Father sent Me, and I live because of the Father, so he who feeds on Me will live because of Me. This is the bread which came down from heaven, not as your fathers ate the manna, and are dead, He who eats this bread will live forever."

Pastor Dave's sermon tied in both the Genesis, Leviticus, Hebrews, and John verses in such a way it was clear that Jesus was Yehoshua, that is the Messiah, and the fulfillment of the Torah prophecies about His coming. They saw that the sacred blood covenant was fulfilled in Jesus shedding His blood on the cross in complete propitiation or atonement of our sins now and forever and that future sacrifices were not needed. The body of Jesus was the bread of life, the manna from heaven sent by the Father to atone for our sins and to unite the nations of the world to the Father through Jesus.

Although salvation comes from the Jews because Jesus and all His disciples were all Jewish, God sent Paul (also known as Saul), a Pharisee, the most Jewish of all the Jews, to spread the gospel to the Gentiles and that the Gentiles (nations) had been grafted into and with their Jewish brethren. God's favorite city is Jerusalem, and His people are still the Jews, but because of His great mercy, grace and His agape love have been extended to all the nations united under His most precious Son, Jesus, the Messiah Yehoshua. The Gentile nations were now grafted into the Jewish family tree through Jesus. After the sermons, we prayed together and were able to unite our groups into one community and one facility.

We also had about a dozen individuals from the town who were mainly Bosnian Muslims. They moved into the town and were offered one of the meeting rooms or the basement room to hold their services. They did not accept us at first, but when they saw that the only people who accepted them in town were the members of the three combined churches, they started meeting on Friday night or Saturday morning or afternoon at one of the church's meeting rooms. The men of each of the families had been placed into concentration camps by the Serbian government during the Balkan Wars, and they survived their incarceration. Two were brothers and three others were cousins who brought their families to the village when they retired. They sold their homes in the neighboring state and moved to our town because they were friends of Moe and Irene. Moe and Irene had been missionaries to Bosnia during the war years of the 1990s, when they brought relief supplies with medical and dental teams for four years, between 1993 and 1997, due to the war. They personally helped them when they came to the USA as refugees, when they had no means of support. They developed a close personal bond between the families and had mutual respect of one another.

It was the Christians (both Catholic and Protestant groups) who assisted them and comforted them to meet their needs. They showed them that God's love was extended to all His children, both those of the flock and those He considered temporarily lost. They knew we strongly believed and practiced God's love for all His peoples and all His nations, even those who were misguided by power and greed. They, too, became believers and part of our united congregation. Vinko, a Croatian, and his wife, Vlatka, also became very close friends of Bosnians over the years.

The Catholics were down to approximately eighty regular members and about a hundred others at Christmas and Easter services. Their pastor was Father Jake, and most of the regular members were Charismatic Catholics who were over seventy years of age, with about fifteen under that age, but these were over forty years old.

The Protestant group was down to about fifty-five active members, but they were mainly evangelical Christians. Their shepherd was Pastor Dave, who retired from a large church to this small flock of dedicated Christians, for which some had been members of his other church. What bound them together was their unwavering love of the God of Abraham and respect for all the children of God. There was no animosity among the groups, who showed love to all, even those who continually harassed them and picked on them with hateful and ignorant words and actions. They stood up for each of the other group members when it mattered and consoled those being abused.

Many of the regular members had made a Tres Dias weekend, which fostered Christian beliefs focused upon the important issue that mattered or united us, such as Abba Father, Jesus the Son, and the Holy Spirit or Comforter. The traditions or ceremonies or how we worship are not important. Religion is not important, but our relationship with God, Jesus, and His Spirit and our walk with Him are what matters. The combined groups within the churches became a community within the village. As time passed, we prayed and worshipped together. We met one another's needs, shared our resources, time, and talents. We prayed daily to give us strength and for God to use us mightily in His service and in unity.

The group was not only a mixture of religions but also of social status, veterans, patriots, homeless, rich, poor, conservatives, moderates, and a couple of enlightened liberals. Individual respect of a person's worth and being a child of God were more important than status and worldly beliefs. The group's focus was upon the commonality in Yahweh, the Father, the God of Abraham, and the creator of all that exists. Although this group made up approximately 7 percent of the town, they alone assisted, fed, housed, and cared for those in need and the sick. When individuals were healed through prayer or the laying on of hands, they were further harassed by the townsfolk. The one tried to charge church members for practicing medicine without a license.

Pastor Dave noted that Rabbi Maskil had been one of the most persecuted of the Jews in the town. They ridiculed him for his prophetic abilities and his belief that Jesus was the prophesized Messiah. In June of 2016, he made a prophetic statement about Trump winning the election over Clinton when the polls said she had a 97 percent chance of winning. He stated Trump was going to win and would declare Jerusalem as the capital of Israel. He also stated that Trump meant "one who blows the trumpet in Zion and over the threshing floor of David." When a newsman printed the prophecy, the townsfolk made great fun of him. However, when Trump won, they blamed him for swaying the outcome. So they would jeer him, point fingers, and holler out, "Prophet, Prophet, will it rain today?" Rabbi Maskil would not respond other than saying, "When God gives the watchman a revelation, it is his responsibility to inform or warn the people on the events that will unfold. I am only the messenger, one crying out in the wilderness of the unsaved."

Later, when Trump declared that America acknowledged Jerusalem as the capital of Israel, the same folks stepped up their taunting. He would only respond with, "For it is written, 'God raises up leaders for such a time as this' or 'God is in control.'" The villagers would walk by him and say, "Where's your telephone to God? What does your God predict for us today?" The rabbi would only smile and respond, "Come to church and you will find out."

The main problems in our town was the big disconnect between the youngest and oldest generations, that is, those in their teens, twenties, and thirties with those being over sixty years old. The younger generations looked at the elderly with animosity because the government and the liberal media kept telling the people the social security system would go bankrupt. They attempted to shore it up with massive tax increases, which hurt small businesses and drove the rich away to countries with low tax rates and who gave up their US citizenship.

The younger generations would say as they walked by us in the park, "Why don't you guys just die? You're bankrupting our pension fund!" Or "You are too old and should be dead by now. Why you don't just die and do us a favor?" Or "Stop taking up our resources, you bunch of useless pieces of crap!" The youngsters and their parents had no respect for their elders. We even heard two teenagers talking in the park about how they could not wait for their own grandparents and parents to die so they could inherit their money and start enjoying their life.

Despite all the taunting, abuses, and continued ridicule by the younger adults and children, the older churchgoing men and women just continued to love upon these misguided villagers. We just loved upon them and told them how much Jesus and the Father loved them and how much He missed them, but much to no avail, because the taunting only escalated. Moe would say to the others when they became flustered, "I'm a duck, quack, quack. Just like a duck when the water rolls off its back, so do the nasty comments roll off my backs."

The veterans took a lot more abuse than we did, except for Rabbi Maskil. The younger generations did not like the military for the wars in which they served. They saw the wars as a needless expenditure of resources that could have been used by them for their pleasures. They had freedom but could not understand that freedom must be fought for and it does not come without a price. They believed in the old 1970s songs that "freedom was just another word for nothing left to lose." They were just preoccupied with self-indulgence and self-gratification.

Our church members believed in Ephesians 3:16 being the "Ramos" (living the Word) and not only in the "Logos" (just knowing or believing the Word) of God. Living the scriptures was difficult in an antagonistic society where freedom of religion once existed. Society now was about "freedom from religion," and if it feels good, just do it. The Judeo-Christian principles were now considered antiquated by the world and just too unreasonable to follow because it impaired their freedom.

Pastor Dave taught us, "Love increases faith, while faith works through love. To achieve a state of piety is having the faith in God and demonstrating one's agape love, as noted in Mathew 25:31. If we cannot succeed at love, then we cannot succeed in anything. We need the courage to trust and obey through love, by faith, and with God's grace. Love needs to be the motivating factor by the love of God and the love of the neighbor. We have the power of choice to love or not obey."

We walked in the peace of God, as Jesus said in John 14:26–27. As Pastor Dave often said, "We walk by faith and not by sight or by feelings. Feelings are the devil's domain." We believed that one did not change one's circumstances by worrying about them, so we just put our shoulders to the plow and did the Lord's work.

As we walked along, we saw the local bully and his two teenage sons. They were picking on one of the homeless vets as he sat on the park bench. Then we walked over to them and asked Billy, the bully, how we could help him. Billy told us that we and the rest of the ancients should stop feeding these derelicts and maybe they would go back to where they came from. The rabbi told Billy that this man was a war hero who made a great sacrifice for our county and now many from our country had abandoned him or others in the same situation. "But our church will not abandon them," he said. "Our church wants to honor their sacrifice and dedication to our nation.

We desire to do the work of the Lord to meet their needs until they can provide for themselves and get back on their feet. Our church is just being obedient to God by servicing those who serviced our country to protect our liberties."

Rabbi Maskil looked at Billy and said to him, "Since you are Greek, the Lord has a few words for you. Dikaioma and Krisis!"

Billy looked at him and said, "What the hell does that mean? I do not speak Greek."

So, the rabbi said, "It is written in Revelation 16:7 and 19:2. A decision of judgment has been decreed and a separation has been made leading to that judgment. You are the son of Belial, but it is not too late. Repent and ask for forgiveness to avoid your judgment. What a powerful name is Jesus!"

At that, Billy said to his sons, "Let's go, before he starts giving us more religious crap." With that, he and his sons departed.

As we sat down with him, we talked for a few minutes. Then we said to him, "Don't listen to bullies like him. In my father's house, there is a place for you and us. For it is written, 'We must pray for those who spitefully use us. Who the son sets free is free indeed.' You are free to do what the Lord has planned for you. You help the other homeless vets by helping the church provide for them, by assisting in feeding them and finding a place to stay. You spend half your day cooking for others. You are doing God's will, in that what may appear to be menial tasks for you are a very big thing for others and for our God." This perked him up, and so I said to him, "I'm hungry, and would you be so kind to join us for lunch? We do not like to eat alone." The vet was glad to join us because he, too, was hungry. We walked over to the various vendors in the park and grabbed a few burgers and fries.

It was funny to see the various people from the village in the park on this beautiful spring day. The temperature was in the lower seventies and very comfortable. What I did notice was that when-ever the villagers came near any of the church members, the vets, or the homeless, they pretended not to notice or looked away in the opposite direction. The only exceptions were the poor villagers of the town, whom the church members continuously assisted in their needs. They were so grateful and thankful. They would often come to church, but not every Sunday at first. As love permeated in their souls, their hearts became full of God's grace and forgiveness.

As a group of us from the church sat on the park benches, we talked about how the world had changed and, especially, how our country had changed. After four years of growth under the Trump administration, the wealth of the American international conglomerates came pouring back into the USA. With repatriating the overseas funds and the abolishment of the foreign tax credit, the incentives to keep operations overseas were removed. Investment in US businesses was at an all-time level, and unemployment was down to 2.9 percent in January of 2020. Specialty trades were at an all-time high, and labor had to be imported from Canada, South America, European countries, India, Philippines, and Ireland. Prosperity was at an all-time high, and the economy was booming throughout 2019 and early 2020. The stock market broke the thirty-thousand mark.

The swamp and their mouthpieces kept attacking the Trump administration with various false charges in an attempt to impeach him. Before he took office, the democratic leadership vowed to impeach him. They started with Russia-gate, then used plants from the FBI and the various administrative positions even within the White House. The plants and press twisted everything he said and did. The fake news media and the Silicon Valley groups would criticize the administration for whatever they did and would criticize them for things they should have done but did not. They even censored free speech by knocking individuals off the Internet, Twitter, and Google. Thanks to the ACLU and the evangelical Christians, the swamp lost all battles with the Trump administration and the economy just kept getting better. Despite this, Trump's approval rating kept on increasing.

The swamp decided to find a way to ruin the economy just to get to Trump and to test methods as to how to control and reduce the population. Through the WHO and other affiliated worldwide groups controlled by them, they decided to claim that simple virus was worse than other previous viruses. For more than a decade, between ten thousand and sixty thousand Americans had died from various annual viruses during the flu season each year. After they lost their last attempt to impeach, this mysterious virus from China was to affect the world. A virus that a world agency had a pattern on and a virus from an area of China that was their "research laboratory" for biochemical warfare. Suddenly, the world had to quarantine to stop the spread of this virus. When Trump stopped travel to and from China, the Mideast, and Europe, the swamp criticized his administration. When other countries followed suit, then they criticized him for moving too late. Despite the fact that the federal government had given the states billions of dollars over the past ten years to staff and stock each state's Department of Emergency Preparedness, most states were not prepared or had any emergency plan for such a pandemic even though they had dealt with such a situation with Ebola. They criticized the federal government for not moving fast enough even though Trump dispatched much assistance and recruited businesses to pitch in and develop supplies and equipment.

The Democratic Party was taken over by extreme liberals like Pocahontas, communists who called themselves progressives. In 2020, radical Muslims also became elected and constantly attacked issues of helping Israel and the Christian conservative values. In 2018 they took control of the House of Representatives, and Nancy Pelosi became speaker of the House once again. They constantly attempted to impeach President Trump even after many expensive special prosecutors and Russia-gate failed to find enough evidence of collusion. After the 2020 elections, things started to spiral into chaos. The Democrats, for four years, tried to impeach the president with fake news, with false witnesses, by using allegations as facts without evidence, and by funding protests to erode Trump's political base. Although the House impeached him, the Senate exonerated him by exposing the false testimonies and truth. All these efforts only exposed their hideous plots of hatred and power. The swamp tried to fight back but were not only exposed but also damaged. Several states changed the voting rules to hide them stuffing the ballots with illegal votes.

After much animosity, recounts, court battles, and voter verifications, even though President Trump won the 2020 elections, the Electoral College, due to the ballot stuffing, voted Biden as the president. The Republicans did not gain control of the House, but they barely kept control of the Senate. The atmosphere became very heavy. The Democrats, certain career bureaucrats, the fake news moguls, the tech media executives, and Antifa refused to not acknowledge the loss of the Senate, and they vowed that there would be no peace and there would be a price to pay. The battles for the presidency ragged on for months. Texas and other states discussed leaving the United States to form their own Conservative Southern States of America.

Three months later, in the spring of 2021, President Trump, Vice President Pence, many former cabinet members, Republican senators and representatives, and the former secretary of state were all assassinated at the same time while attending a party function at Trump Towers in New York. It was a massive explosion that blew out all the upper three floors of Trump Tower, where over 150 conservative supporters and wealthy individuals perished. There were so much finger-pointing going on; the Republicans were blaming the Democrats, the FBI, and other government agencies, but nothing came of it. The media suppressed any criticism of the new administration. It was just the opportunity the progressive communist Democrats needed to ram through their agenda and unravel immigration and socialist policies. The progressive (Communist) teamed up with newly elected extreme liberals in 2021 to promote open borders, free college education, free medical care through Medicare, abolishing the Electoral College, a guaranteed job for everyone, and a 70 percent tax rate on everyone earning over $400,000.

The Speaker of the House immediately gained absolute control of the House and Senate whereby the Democratic governors appointed Democrats to replace their Republican predecessors, which meant that the democratic socialist communist now controlled all three branches of the government. The media down-played everything concerning Republican accusations and defined them as conspiracy theories. They blamed Russia and the extreme right-wing groups. By 2022, they had repealed much of what the Trump administration had done. They tore down the wall, opened the borders, abolished ICE, and eliminated restrictions and immigration laws in this country. Anyone could come into our country, get on social security, disability, or welfare. The culture of the country changed dramatically, especially in the larger sanctuary cities. The various ethnic groups clustered in various sections of the larger cities, like Boston, Los Angeles, Chicago, Miami, New York, Baltimore, Philadelphia, and San Francisco. Just like London and Paris, large Mideastern Muslim populations gathered in specific sections of the city, and even the police would not enter their sections of the city. They ignored our laws and established their own Sharia laws and courts and executed their own judgments within their sector, just as they had done in France and the United Kingdom. They brought over with them their two or three wives and many children. Some even had as many as six wives. Many of the younger men did not appear to have any gainful employment and seemed to be hanging out at their local coffee houses all day and evening, talking, or talking on their cell phones. Many of the middle-aged men infiltrated key organizations worldwide, like the UN peacekeeping forces, controlling UN refugee camps and key NPO groups. The main purpose was to spread hatred for the USA, democracies, Christians, and Jews. They call them "haters" of tolerance, diversity, or just racist.

The population grew by over 120 million in just six short years, of which the Mideastern groups accounted for 20 percent of the increase. The other larger population increase came from South America, Central America, China, Ukraine, Ireland, Russia, and India. These new immigrants were mainly elderly, sick, or young adults.

Last year, the new socialist-progressive administration attempted to confiscate the wealth of the private pension funds by merging them into a government-controlled fund, just like Cypress did nearly twenty-five years earlier. This was a failed attempt to shore up the social security system, which was fast being depleted due to the new immigrants who were over sixty-seven.

The progressive liberals also attempted to transfer the wealth of the individuals who had more than five million dollars in the banks or investment house and use the funds to pay down the national debt. This caused a significant outflow of funds to various countries. The mega-rich and the multinational corporations panicked and started to transfer their funds to Ireland, Switzerland, United Kingdom, and Belgium by shipping products to foreign affiliates and collecting the funds in those countries.

Many of the very wealthy Americans (the 1 percent of America's richest) moved to other countries like Ireland, England, Australia, Austria, Germany, Israel, Brazil, Portugal, Switzerland, and a few private islands in the Pacific. They sold their American businesses on the stock market and took the technical and financial brainpower with them and opened businesses in their new countries. They gave up their American citizenship and took on the citizenship of their host country. They systematically transferred their wealth out of the United States so that in three years their fortunes were in their new country. Savings and investments plummeted while unemployment increased. The new policy of a guaranteed job for every resident meant the old WPA was back in business and union construction jobs decreased due to public works projects now being done by the new JGP, or Jobs Guarantee Program, passed in 2023. By 2026, private sector jobs now only accounted for 28 percent of the workforce. Individual entrepreneurs were discouraged from starting businesses because they could not pay the $25-per-hour minimum wage and because of the severe 12 percent employer payroll taxes to fund Medicare, free schooling or training, and the JGP initiative. Many businesses in the construction noticed that they were funding their competition in the public works and environmental sectors.

The new progressive socialist administration drove out these individuals by passing new social programs and funding them with heavy tax increases on those earning more than $250,000. The tax rate jumped to 70 percent of earnings and the elimination of all deductions once one earned more than $500,000. The labor laws were passed, which increased the cost for business over five employees. Employers had to provide employees more than four weeks of paid vacation days after three years of employment in addition to the other paid time off, such as twelve holidays and thirty sick days. Minimum wages were initially increased to $20 per hour, with a one-dollar-per-hour increase each year for five years.

After experiencing the best growth in the economy from 2016 through 2020, the nation was in a financial tailspin due to the socialist programs and laws. Tax revenues dropped off dramatically and the national debt doubled during the past six years. As China and Russia grew strong, our nation was weakened.

The World Trade Organization and the World Bank no longer considered the US dollar as being the international trade currency and created its own trade currency instead. All nations had to exchange its currency for this new currency and had to place on deposit at the Brussels office transportable assets to back its currency in exchange. The US dollar plummeted and was significantly devalued since trillions of dollars worldwide came flowing back to Brussels and then to the United States. As funds flowed to Brussels, the United States had to transfer hard valuable assets to Brussels to back up those dollars. Gold, silver, platinum, oil, gas, gems, collectibles, and even food products were examples of the types of assets flowing into the Brussels vaults and away from our nation.

Residents, not only citizens, were now guaranteed an initial fifty-two-thousand-dollar income per household, free education, free medical services if they were registered to vote and voted in a prior election. New immigrants were granted voting rights after they were in the country for one year. Welfare and disability rules were relaxed with the passage of a guaranteed minimum income laws in the past two years. These new laws were passed to win votes for the new democratic socialist administration for years to come. The socialist Democrats did whatever they could to guarantee their re-election bid in 2028.

Society's morality among the young was becoming a society of effeminates and Tartarus revelers, especially in the big cities, where the extreme liberals gathered. With a guaranteed income, work became another four-letter work. These young men disdained traditional religion and embraced total freedom, yet they became enslaved in drugs, sex, and perversions of all kinds, as in the days of Noah and Lot.

In 2026 America the great had just reached her point of no return. We were one step away from becoming a third world nation. The progressives sought to unite America into the newly formed World Government Alliance, which was initiated in Brussels and now had over sixty countries since it was formed in May of 2024. The world was divided into ten districts or regions. The districts set up were the Asian Alliance (headed by China), Russia (the newly formed Union of Soviet Socialist Republics), America (the North and Central American Alliance), South America, United Kingdom, India, Arab Caliphate, the Eastern Mediterranean Coalition (except for Israel), Africa Coalition, and the World Government Alliance (formerly known as the European Union or Common Market). Their target date was January 1, 2030, for the commencement of this new world order. They promoted world unity, equality, and peace.

The new world government was asking the Democrats to become a member of this new world order, and their appointed representative would become the appointed leader, at least initially. The Democrats were putting this solution to voters in the fall election of 2028 to be effective on July 1, 2029. In exchange for joining the new world order, they would have all their debts forgiven. We would no longer be an independent nation; we would be equivalent to a state within the United States, but all of North America and Central America would be one state within the new world order. Each of the ten districts would select their leader from among themselves, and those leaders would appoint the leader of each of the ten districts in the future. It would be the highest form of communism, or rather a dictatorship. The ten members would promulgate all laws, with no appeal process. They would control all military and police forces throughout the world. They would also appoint regional administrators, collect taxes, and approve all government appointments.

They would also merge all religions into a new world religion called Chrislam, with the members of the Arab Caliphate being the initial pope-like head. Since Pope Francis, the largest denomination in the world was promoting unity of all religions under a new doctrine that gave Jesus a back seat as a prophet and as a good person and not as the only begotten Son of God. To try to attract Israel into the union, the pledged peace and rebuilding of the new temple of Salomon, whereby the Arabs would concede an area near the temple mount.

As a matter of fact, they preached that all people were the sons and daughters of God and not only Jesus. We were moving into absolute control by demigods. The leader would be granted a seat of the new world order to control the religious doctrine being preached throughout the world.

In the countries that had already signed up for this, they systematically took control of all media, Internet, hospitals, clinics, utilities, banks, distribution centers, and major industries. They started their persecution of what they called hate groups, which included skinheads, patriots, Jews, Christians, and any other group that opposed them. Jews and evangelical Christians exited the country and flew to Israel, while other Christians went to Italy, Australia, South America, England, and Greece.

THE SEVENTY DAYS
OF THE WORD

We would gather at the church every Wednesday at sun-down. We would refer to the church facility as Bema. We did this because we did not want the young misfits to know where we gathered. If we said, "Let's meet at the church at seven," then the boys would go there and heckle us all night. So the rabbi started calling our meeting place Bema in the park, which in Hebrew tradition referred to the judgment seat of Joshua. This would indicate for us to meet on Wednesday a half-hour before sun-down. He also coined our meeting at sunrise as meeting a Zikkaron in the park, which actually came from Malachi 3:16 and meant "the book of remembrance," so that we would remember to come and worship Yahweh and Yeshua first thing in the morning. This avoided our being hassled by the young liberal vagrants who would be search-ing for us in the park but could not find us because the park was so large and wrapped around the entire lake.

It was at the midweek prayer service and about 120 of us were gathered at the church at sunset on Wednesday, April 21, 2027, when the prophetic word came to us gathered to worship the Lord. The mean age of the faithful gathered that day was seventy-seven years, but they ranged from mid-forties to upper eighties. Despite our age, we felt like we were in our fifties, still healthy and independent in most cases, although some were in wheelchairs or used walkers and canes. We had just finished our songs of praise unto the Lord and Yahweh. We prayed for continued unity among the brethren and for God to use us mightily and powerfully in service to Him and our fellow man. Many yearned to be used by God and would be called into service above and beyond what we considered trivial in what we were doing to help those in need in the village. This prayer was always included in all our gatherings. Our worship team just finished singing, "I give my life away so You can use me," and "Here I am, here I stand," and as we contemplated on the words "Take my life, take my heart as a living sacrifice," Rabbi Maskil stood up and told those gathered that Yahweh had given him a word but one of the other members of the congregation had to give a word first. He then looked around the congregation, and he focused upon Irene, who was beaming and appeared to have the anointing on her. So he asked Irene to come up front and give the word that was given to her by Abba Yahweh.

So the rabbi placed a chair in the front middle aisle of the church and asked the congregation to sing one last song, and he led them in the song that was on his heart. He started off the song entitled "When It's All Been Said and Done" by Robin Mark, and the congregation sang from the heart:

> When it's all been said and done
> There is just one thing that matters
> Did I do my best to live for truth?
> Did I live my life for you?
>
> When it's all been said and done
> All my treasures will mean nothing
> Only what I've done
> For love's reward
> Will stand the test of time.
>
> Lord, your mercy is so great
> That you look beyond our weakness
> And find purest gold in miry clay
> Turning sinners into saints

I will always sing your praise
Here on earth and ever after
For you've shown me heavens my true home
When it's all been said and done
You're my life when life is gone
When it's all been said and done
There is just one thing that matters,
Did I do my best to live for truth?
Did I live my life for you?

Then Pastor Forshia went up and said that the Lord whispered to her and said she needed to play on his old tape player a John Polce song. She played "Do You Love Me Enough?" As everyone listened, they meditated on the words of the song, and what stood out the most for me and our congregation were the words "Do you love me enough?" and "Can you walk the walk I walked for you?" We were all mesmerized by the words of Jesus's love for us and contemplated whether we would be strong at our old age to walk the walk for Jesus. We were all great at talking the talk, but could we be as obedient to the Father as Jesus or as Abraham, Noah, or Moses against all odds or uncertainties? Pastor David always told us that the Bible states, "Obedience is far better than sacrifice. God tested Abraham and faith grows through testing and through use. God reward faith through grace and the just shall live by faith. Also, Abraham was an unselfish person and obedience is an unselfish act for God."

Our congregations had been praying for God to use us in a mighty way, and we thought that by loving upon the residence of this village, despite their abusing us and ridiculing us, we were accomplishing the task God had set before us. We always wondered if God would ask us to do anything other than what we were doing.

Pastor David got up and said, "God wants each of us to ask ourselves several questions: 'Are you who you think you are?' God sought throughout the kingdom for one righteous man. God welcomes the prayers of the righteous, and nothing happens without prayers. Are we truly righteous men and women? Are our prayers from the heart? Do we genuinely love Jesus enough to walk His walk? Are we obedient to God's will, and would we stand up for Him, or would we run like the disciples did in the garden? Do we fear being tested by God even though we pray for God to use us mightily? Would we leave our homeland like Abram or build an ark like Noah where there is no water? Or even go back to Egypt, where certain death awaits, like Moses? Like Peter before the resurrection, what will we do when the trials come? Will we deny Him or even curse Him? Will we be afraid and scatter like the other disciples? All here have prayed for God to use us mightily. Will we respond, 'Yes, Lord, send me'? Will we go and carry our cross to our death if asked?"

Immediately there was an awesome presence and stillness in the church like none ever experienced by the group. The silence lasted over thirty minutes, but it seemed only like five minutes as each of us went into a heavenly meeting with the Lord and Abba Yahweh. We all had "the encounter," and we, in part, had the exact same message and, in part, had a message specific for each one of us.

At the end of basking with the Lord, Irene spoke these prophetic words from Him: "My faithful chosen ones, you are one of My remnant people who have stood by Me through many trials, persecutions, ridicule, and sacrifice. I know you love Me even though you are of many backgrounds, tongues, races, and nations. My Son said He is also pleased that you did not desert Him or betray Him during adversity. You know I love the world so much that I gave My only begotten Son so that the world will be united unto Me in the fulfilment of Scripture. His suffering was to unite My chosen people with the nations, but My people and then the nations rejected Him as My chosen people rejected Me. Through My Son, the nations have been grafted onto My chosen people.

"I have given you a message that is for all the faithful, and I have given you a message that is solely unto you to use when the time is right, and you will understand the message on the seventieth day.

"You must gather at sunrise on that day, and I will reveal the final message. So continue to be faithful when all is said and done. As I did not spare My only Son, I will ask you to solely bear the burden of this village so that they may believe that I and My Son sent you. Know that I am with you despite all odds, like Gideon, like Moses, and like David. Many of you will be spared like John, but you must not fear but be courageous like Joshua. I will strengthen you in faith and in body; the lame shall walk, the blind shall see, and the deaf shall hear during the days of peril, and you will overcome all obstacles. I will make your mind keen and will give unto you a plan to 'stand your ground' on behalf of this village and as a witness to Israel, America, and the whole world. Out of every nation, I have called a remnant to stand their ground on my behalf. Gideon called the ten thousand, but only three hundred went into battle. Your village will run in fear, but the seventy will stand alone and hold the ground. I want you to remember LOT, that is, 'listen, obey, and trust.' Trust only in Me and My Word.

"You will recall all that I have told you tonight and during the next seventy days, I will reveal a plan to stand your ground. You will not falter, for you will know that I will be with you throughout the six days of testing. On the seventh day, you will rest. Soon thereafter, you will rest in Me, and I in you, for I have prepared a place for you.

"Focus upon Me and My Son, sing songs of praise, lift your banners high, and blast My songs of praise so all can hear. Blast forth My Word, which will be a burning sword unto their hearts, and which will drive them mad with anger and confusion. They will fall into My trap and not understand. They will rage like a mad dog and be cut down by My Spirit, for it is written, 'Not by power, not by might, but by My Spirit,' says the Lord.

"The world believes you are feeble, old, and should be discarded. That is why I have chosen you, and that is why they will believe in My power just like in the days of Moses.

"They will not forget what will transpire here until the end of the age, which will occur soon begin hereafter. Although they will forget your names, they will not forget the sacrifice you made in standing your ground for them and for all new believers. They will change their hearts and flock back to Me, and this will unite My chosen ones with My Son's chosen followers again. They will know that I am your God and that you are My sacrificial children. I will melt their hearts of stone and place My Spirit once again into their hearts, which they had driven out in favor of what the world offers."

The Lord continued to say, "I have asked for more than 180 years, that My people humble themselves and repent. I will hear their cries, but except for the remnant, most have fallen away, so I have started the birth pains. I have sent the blood moons, the alignment of the planets and stars, and other warning, yet to little avail. I have placed the TAV upon My righteous. Warn those who remain, as it is written in the books, they are not to take the mark of he who is to rule the earth in the latter half of the end-time week. For that which has been is that which shall be.

"These next seventy days, you need to pray, pray, and pray so that you do not fall into the temptation of Peter, the rock. Gather here at this sanctuary of hope. Strengthen one another before the hour of trial and understand that I am with you. Know that before the hour of battle will begin, I will strengthen each one of you as I will it. When the call goes out, go in unison to answer the call. Go together in unity and in might and be courageous. Stand your ground with the leaders, and in Me have Trust without borders, because I am with you and I will not let you down. Follow My instructions to the last tittle. Although some will perish, not all will perish, so that My glory will be known, and all will see that I am your God. Those who perish will not die but will be with Me for all eternity.

"During the next seventy days, I will give one person complete and detailed instructions as to the tasks he or she must do. In addition, I will also, on the seventh day of each week, at seven o'clock, give instructions to the leadership of the congregation, and to the leaders I will handpick to lead specific tasks and give specific counsel. You will also need to draw from your experiences. However, look to My Word and My truth. Write down My Word and My instructions so that you can commence executing your assigned tasks with vigor and with precision when the time comes. You are the chosen seventy elders of the new covenant of Israel, and among you I have chosen officers, and your leadership needs to be sensitive to the others who have not been chosen for leadership but have been chosen for a very important task. You need not be concerned. Treat the task as doing it unto Me and for the glory of the kingdom. No task is too menial and equally as great, just as the body of Christ. All have their unique function and must work in harmony together. Otherwise, the whole body will suffer. Gather daily at sunrise and at sunset for the next seventy days. Do not complain as did the Israelites, for your murmuring will cause you pain. The staff of Moses cannot save you from the pain if you do.

"You need not prepare anything until day 70, and you will have three days to execute the tasks I have directed. During these seventy days, write down what I am instructing you to do. Worry not, whatever you need. No one will resist you at whatever you ask for. People will eagerly volunteer to assist you for these three days, and then they will leave you and you alone will 'stand your ground' for six days, and on the seventh day, they will know that I, Yahweh, am your God, the God of Israel, the only and the original God of America and the creator of the world. Your deeds and those of the other members of the remnants will be known throughout the world, as to how the feeble stood against the might and that My Spirit was with them and they overcame the many thousands.

"My first group message centers on Rabbi Maskil, Pastor Dave, and Father Jake. Rabbi, you will be like Moses in the days of the battles. Take up the staff that I have given to you in the days of your youth and hold it high during the battles yet to come. While the staff is raised high, My people will prevail. If you lower your staff, the enemy's people will prevail.

"To Pastors Dave and Jake, you will be like Aaron and Hur and stand beside Moses in prayer and worship. When his arms tire, you will assist him to hold the staff high so your people will prevail. When you forget or do not assist, one will perish each time the staff drops below the chest. So out of love and out of My Word, do not falter or forget. Pay attention to My instructions. So as the Moabites, Canaanites, Ammonites, Jebusites, Assyrians, Medes, Persians, Babylonians, Egyptians and Chaldeans gather, your rod and staff will prevail against them if you heed My instructions and keep My Word. The fate of your flock rests upon you and your obedience to My instructions and to My Word. For now, tell no one except your spouse, but forbid them to tell anyone else until after day 70. Go home, pray, and arise early tomorrow morning for additional instructions. The mornings will be for prayer and praise, and the evenings for worship, instructions and the Word. Go in peace and fear not. Be courageous and bold. Fear not, for I and My Son will be with you and My Spirit will overshadow you with protection for those who obey My instructions and trust in Me."

There was dead silence for thirty minutes, and one by one they all went home to ponder the meaning of this revelation. Although some questioned why Irene was to have given this prophetic statement as to speaking on behalf of the Lord, they had no doubt that the words were for them individually and as a group. We closed the lights of the church and went home.

The next day, only seventy of us gathered again at the church at sunrise, as instructed, and we started with praise to Yahweh, Jesus, and the Spirit of God. Fifty members were so frightened they did not return. Some later told the pastors that they would not be able to respond to the request for one excuse or another. Some said they could not meet every night. Others said they planned on going to visit family members in other parts of the country. There were a few honest members who said they were afraid to make the sacrifice and endure the trials contemplated because they need to assist their other family members. A few just said nothing and stopped returning to the church. Rabbi Maskil and Pastor Dave were questioned by those members who remained, and Pastor Dave said, "Circumstances don't make us who we are. Circumstances reveal who we are. They reveal the integrity we have. We need to trust in God and obey, and this will produce courage."

Rabbi Maskil stood up and said, "The first thing this morning after my coffee, I heard the Lord whisper to me Isaiah 22. So I went to the Torah and the Bible, and the following words jumped out at me: 'The burden against the Valley of Vision, all your rulers have fled together. All who are found you are bound together. In the Valley of Vision, breaking down the walls and of crying to the mountains, Elam bore the quiver. It shall come to pass that you're your choicest valley which shall be full of chariots and the horseman shall set themselves in array at the gate.' So I prayed for the meaning, and the words I heard in my spirit was, 'Who guides your heart, protect your heart?'

I responded with the words of the song 'As the Deer,' 'You alone are my heart's desire. You alone are my strength and my shield.'"

So we sang in worship that song.

Rabbi Maskil led the praises to Yahweh, Pastor Dave to Jesus, and Father Jake to the Holy Spirit. This lasted for nearly an hour, and then Pastor Dave called upon Irene again, saying, "What instructions have you been given by our Lord?"

Irene said, "No, I do not have any word."

So Pastor Dave prayed, calling up the Holy Spirit to come, and we sang "Come, Holy Spirit" to fill our hearts, our minds, and to instruct us as He wills.

Suddenly, Estelle cried out, "Someone please get me some paper so I can write on. The Lord is downloading a message for me and the tasks I am to perform. I am to give it to Rabbi and to one of the officers to be appointed on the seventh day." She started writing down all that was given to her while the remainder of the congregation sang "Amazing Grace" and "Reckless Love of God," with a few other meditative praise-and-worship songs. We went home just after Estelle said that it was finished and she would make the two copies and present it on the seventh day.

We gathered again that evening about a half-hour before sunset, singing songs of praise and worship. This time Pastor Dave read a passage from the book of Numbers about how Moses selected the seventy elders and from among them leaders of the seventy. No word from the Lord came that evening, and we remembered that He was to give an individual word to one of the seventy and a group word on the seventh day. We were not sure if this meant on Sunday, being the seventh day of the week and a day of rest, or Friday, being the seventh day after the initial word was given. Father Jake read other scriptures from the New Testament, and Rabbi Maskil read words from the Torah from Isaiah. We closed with prayer and sang a John Polce song called "Lord, I Believe," and we all went home.

We gathered every morning and every evening, and one by one a member would receive a word each morning directly from the Lord and they would write it down and give a copy for the leadership while waiting for additional instruction on the seventh day. The people receiving instructions during this first week seemed to have been the three pastors and the women of the congregation. The first of the women who received the individual word were Estelle, Irene, Diane, and Michelle. Everyone wrote down their instructions and made two additional copies to give to the pastors and to the appointed leaders of the seventy as directed.

On Friday evening, being the completion of the seventh day, we eagerly gathered, awaiting the new group message. We commenced again with prayer, praise, and worship. Pastor Dave and Father Jake read from the New Testament. Pastor Dave said, "Faith is to believe what we do not see, and the reward of this faith is to see what we believe." Rabbi Maskil read from the Torah's book of Exodus about the twelve tribes and how they were organized and positioned themselves when they camped. In the middle of his sentence, he stopped and looked at Irene again and said to her, "Oh, daughter of the tribe of Benjamin, you have a word for us." Irene's DNA had verified that she was of the tribe of Benjamin, but the rabbi was never told that. So Pastor Dave set up a chair in the front of the middle aisle, and she sat down while we sang "Spirit of the Living God, all Afresh on Us."

When we stopped singing, Pastor Forshia spoke. "The Lord our God says, 'I have given words to those who are to lift high the banners of love when the trials begin. The rabbi shall lift the staff, but the pastors shall lead the praise and worship with the women I have chosen. As My people marched into battle, the banners of each of the tribes were lifted high and the musicians and the singers sang praise to Me, and as they lifted up their songs of praise, I lifted their strength and their courage. So will it be in the six days of trials. Sing praises and worship to Me during the times of battle, and I will sustain the warriors during the battle. Be vigilant, be dutiful, and do not be afraid. Each of you has been given a song of praise or worship, and each one will give a copy to the pastors and prepare to sing the songs on the designated days of battle. Do not confuse the order. It is especially important that the songs of praise are sung in the order given. However, begin each morning with 'Spirit of the Living God, Fall Afresh on Us' and finish each day's battle with 'Lord I Believe.'"

Michelle stood up and said, "You are to place loudspeakers along the southern road mountain coming to the village for a mile and a half, starting from the church through the mountain passage, and place speakers on the two mountains near the homes of George and Moe. Connect the speaker system so if something should happen, the songs will continue from the other system. Set up communications between the church and the two mountain homes and the positions in which I will instruct you. I will tell the technicians where to position them and where you shall position yourself latter. Be sure you gather your music and music players and organize the songs of praise and worship as I have taught you."

Diane arose and said, "The Lord gave me these words: 'Do not be afraid, sing loud, and do not cease, for when you stop or pause, the evil one will have his people advance on you and they will gain ground. When you sing loud and strong, they will be defeated and flee because of My Word. The songs I have given you come from My holy scriptures. They are to be your shield and defense. My Word will anger the evil one and his people, and they will cause chaos and confusion as well as anger, like a mad dog that is not trained. Start your praising and worship songs when Pastor Dave or Pastor Jake says, "Praise to the Lord all ye people," and do not cease until the battle is won. When you cease, the evil one will gain ground, but while you praise, you will stand your ground.'"

Estelle arose and then said, "Be faithful and be true to My instructions. Avoid despair and chaos. So to have order, you must praise in the order I have given you. Do not fear or allow yourself to panic. Stay true to My Word and I will be your guide and protector. Though at time it may appear bleak, sing louder and sing stronger. The power of the Spirit comes through your praises and the worship using My Word. If you add or subtract from what I have given you, the evil one will advance and one of the seventy will be subtracted."

Irene stood up, saying, "Do as I have instructed and all will be well with you. The battle will end when the last song of praise is completed. Do not repeat any of the songs except those I have given you and sing them in their totality. Learn them during the next sixty-three days. Do not be afraid, for I am with you and I have sent the Comforter to ease your anxieties." Irene then said, "It is finished." And we concluded the service with the Polce songs "Here Is My Servant" and "Lord, I Believe."

The six along with Pastor Dave who were given the songs of praise now understood what they were to do and met daily with the musicians or with CD players to rehearse the songs in their entirety. Many were from the Torah and Old Testament, mainly from the books of Psalms and Proverbs. A few came from the songs written during the first revival in America. There were also several of the modern songs of the recent decade.

During the seventy days, day after day one person was revealed the task he or she must perform and was to share that information only with specific leaders of the seventh day of that week.

Each day a new word was given and written down. The designated leader was given a copy of what they had written during the meeting, and the two who were appointed to become a scribe during each morning at sunrise.

Those selected by the Lord were initially puzzling, but in the end, we would realize that all things came together in a master plan. The leadership included the former military personnel, the town's junkyard owner, a contractor, a person in a wheelchair, a businessman, and a person who was a carpenter who created medieval game toys that the town used in the spring and at harvesttime. If I were to have selected the leaders of a group, most of these individuals, although exceptionally fine people, would not have been selected. I believe God selected them only to prove that He was the power behind any victory, just like Gideon and his three hundred.

God appointed Captain Roger, who had suffered a few strokes and was in a wheelchair, to coordinate communications and surveillance. John, who had been a colonel in the Army Reserves and National Guards and had served in Vietnam, as the defense coordinator. Gary, who was a captain in the Army in Iraq and who also served in the Marines, to accumulate the strategy plans for defense and to oversee one of the main defensive positions. Ralph, a retired engineer, and Vinko, a carpenter, who both were medieval buffs, were to coordinate alternative devices. Moe, a retired business consultant, was to coordinate the logistical planning with Steve, the contractor, and with Henry, the junkyard owner. George, the convenience store and gas station owner, was to coordinate procurement and supplies and work with Moe. The pastors and the rabbi, along with Irene, Michelle, Estelle, Diane, and Hailey, were to coordinate praise and worship, but we initially could not determine what this old, ragtag group was to do for the Lord and how the pieces fit the puzzle.

Week after week we could see bits of the puzzle, but it was only on the morning of the seventieth day of each week did we understand our fate and our calling collectively. Many were troubled and concerned as to how, at their age, they could fulfill their obligations. Others were fearful about the unknown and questioned if they were misunderstanding what God genuinely wanted of them.

The key question everyone was asking themselves was, Whatever we were told, was this to be in the natural or in the spiritual?

A word from the Lord came at our Bema meeting on May 1, and the word was, "Beware of the return of 'En Esure' and the 'Ein Zippori in Galilee of the days of old.' It will soon be like the days of Noah and Lot." At first, we were puzzled, but the rabbi informed us that the wickedness of those days of old would soon be upon us. That the spirt of the Leviathan had been released during the birth pains of the end-time. Rabbi also stated that we need to watch God's patterns. From the time of the Torah to Jesus or Yeshua, the prophets told of Christ's coming, and from the arrival of Christ to His second coming, the prophecies would be all fulfilled. Daniel tells us about what and when they will be fulfilled. Revelations talks about what the judgments and signs will be. The scriptures proceed forward to Christ and reverts to the beginning. Jesus said, "I am the Alpha and the Omega. As it was in the beginning, so will it be at the end with the coming of Yeshua and the new Jerusalem."

It was during Memorial Day in May when madness started to occur. On the East Coast, an enormous wave 100 feet high swept from Maine to the Florida Keys and the islands. It also caused much damage in the northern portion of South America and Central America. It was caused by an eruption of a volcano at the Canary Islands. Many coastal African and European countries were also affected. It flooded the coastal cities and all the Caribbean Islands. Within three hours of that event, another 150-foot wave hit the West Coast from Alaska to the tip of South America. This was caused by an earthquake in the Pacific Rim and a significant movement of the plates in the Pacific Ocean. Again, all the coastal cities and towns were affected. The western countries and the United States were in turmoil. Many Asian countries were also affected.

The spirit of Leviathan (the twisted spirit) was unleashed. In the so-called sanctuary cities throughout the country, ethic riots broke out among the immigrants, or so it seemed at that time. The military was called out because the local and state police forces were not able to contain the clashes and it spread throughout the cities. People were being murdered by the tens of thousands, with the police and military being prime targets of those rebelling. The police and the military strength were significantly reduced by "defunding the police movement" in the early twenties. Later, this proved to have been a plot designed by ISISA (which is ISIS America) leaders to spark turmoil, which started the uprising.

Mass exodus was occurring during the first two weeks of June from the big cities. The wealthy and the upper middle class were leaving their homes in the large cities and sought refuge in their summer or winter vacation homes. From Los Angeles to Boston to Miami to New Orleans to Chicago, the riots and turf battle occurred daily.

Then on the day of the equinox, June 21, a full-fledged war broke out, and ISISA was at its forefront. The refugees from the Middle East, from Syria, Iraq, Iran, Lebanon, Yemen, and Afghanistan, and those from Egypt, Sudan, and Libya in Africa, who were admitted to the sanctuary cities as a result of the liberals winning control of the government since 2020, commenced fighting as a unit and taking over major portions of the major cities. Over twelve million of the so-called refugees came from those countries. What the government did not take note of was that from 2022 to 2026, nearly 80 percent of the refugees from these countries were single males between the ages of sixteen and twenty-five sent by ISIS to tear apart this country. They were trained soldiers since they were ten years old. They were also trained in causing dissension and sowing the seeds of rebellion among other ethnic groups. Many of these fighters were able to join the military forces under the path to citizenship. During the initial phase of the conflict, many of those Americans killed were killed by the ISISA force within our military. Due to the equality laws passed, they were able to obtain high military ranks by playing the ethnic or race card when promotions were being handed out. Several military facilities in New England and California had been taken over by these groups, giving them access to much of the weapons and equipment that were distributed to other ISISA fighters in these sanctuary cities.

Despite the conflicts going on in the large cities, our little town just went on as normal because it did not affect them. None of the town's sons or daughters were in the military; therefore, they were not directly affected. Despite the calamity occurring in the major cities, most of the townsfolk were just going about their business as if this were just about to end or that it would not occur in our town or our state.

The town was preparing for the Fourth of July fireworks celebrations, and the pyrotechnic team had just arrived, today being the first of July, and they looked over the areas to commence setting up their equipment. They normally would be setting up on the lakeside of the park, but they thought maybe another location should be considered. The townsfolk were setting up the tents and food booths along the park perimeter near the town's boulevard. They also set up the various games, including the medieval catapults, for the festivities in the park. This had been a tradition in our village for over sixty years.

It was about ten o'clock that morning when a herd of over one hundred deer from the south came rampaging through the center of the town, using the main road through the town, heading north. In addition, behind the deer were nearly two dozen moose. Within ten minutes after the moose, several hundred rabbits came hopping through the town on the road, going north. One of the teenagers made a comment, "The deer and the moose are running away from the attack bunnies," and they just laughed it off. This had never occurred in the past. They usually stayed to the south woods or followed the river stream to the east of the mountains or to the west of the mountains. An hour later, tens of thousands of different types of birds flew over our town, heading north. There were so many it became dark as midnight for almost ten minutes. Still, the townsfolk went about their business.

It was just after one in the afternoon when thousands of cars, trucks of all sizes, SUVs, campers, buses of all kinds, including school buses, came parading through the town, heading north. They arrived bumper to bumper nonstop for over an hour and a half. Still, no one paid any mind to these anomalies except our church group.

It wasn't until three o'clock that afternoon that the villagers started to wonder. We were sitting on the park bench just off the boulevard when hundreds of US military vehicles, jeeps, personnel carriers, tanks, trucks towing equipment, and other cars, pickup trucks, campers, buses, and vans with military personnel in them came storming through the center of town at forty miles an hour for more than an hour. There must have been over three thousand vehicles just pouring through this town. At first, the villagers thought they were going to the large northern city for their annual Fourth of July parade. At the rear of this caravan, several military jeeps and trucks stopped in the square in front of the mayor's office.

The soldiers disembarked from their vehicles, and guards were posted in front of the mayor's office while three officers went inside the office. Fifteen minutes later, the major and the three officers went over to the police station, and soon thereafter, they walked over to the town's radio station, followed by all the six police officers in the town. So we turned our dial on our "boom box" to the radio station number to see what was going on. The station was playing a George M. Coen song from World War I, "It's a Grand Old Flag," and then the announcer said, "We are interrupting this broadcast for a special emergency announcement by the mayor." Then the mayor spoke and said, "There will be a special town meeting at the park's stage where graduations are normally held. Please, everyone must gather there at five o'clock. Please tell your neighbors immediately. The siren from the fire station will go off at 4:30 p.m., and please go around your neighborhood, telephone your family and friends in the village to attend this important meeting. All residents and all visitors must attend. This meeting is critical to all. Therefore, you have about half an hour after the siren goes off. I ask all town employees, all depart-ments, and all town volunteers to report to the bandstand at the park immediately after you call your family regarding this message.

I am asking all business owners or managers to close their businesses until after the town's meeting, so all can attend. This meeting is especially important and mandatory. I thank you in advance for your full cooperation."

Now everyone was abuzz as to what was so important to have a town meeting. The policemen, firemen, public works department, recreation department, and all the other town employees met at the bandstand in the park, and they went out to the various businesses just in case they did not hear the radio announcement. People were going around the town like chicken with their heads cut off. At 4:15 p.m., cars and trucks came pouring in and the parking lots filled up faster than a Black Friday shopping event. The siren went off for ten minutes, and more people were directed to the soccer field for additional parking.

We moseyed on down to the stage area, where the recreation department had set up hundreds of chairs for people to sit down on, which meant the meeting was going to last more than fifteen minutes. The six of us got ourselves a front-row seat. The siren kept blasting until five o'clock, then stopped. The mayor, the police chief and the entire police force, the fire chief and the entire fire personnel (including all the volunteers), all the town's department heads, and the Army captain, along with six of his officers, went onto the stage and sat down.

The mayor stood up and went to the microphone with an overly concerned look on his face and said, "Thank you for attending this very special meeting. I would like to introduce Captain Mark Allworth of the state National Guard's command center. Please pay attention closely to his message and instructions."

Captain Mark came to the podium in an a typical military fashion, and he addressed the villagers, saying, "Thank you for attending this meeting. I am here on behalf of the governor of the state to inform you that things are not going well in the big cities and mayhem has now spilled over to the rest of the rural portions of the states. The governor has just declared martial law throughout the state, and I am in command in this region. The mayor, police, and other town officials are under my command.

"We have a division of the National Guard holding back more than ten thousand ISISA troops. They had taken control of many major cities in the area and have acquired assets from the surrounding military bases. Luckily, they have not acquired many military planes. We were able to relocate them in the northern portion of the state. We have taken many military assets with us, but we were not able to take all of them, and the enemy has quite a few assets in their possession. They are attacking the smaller cities and villages surrounding the larger cities. Our nearly two hundred crack troops are fighting to stall ISISA from advancing north along this very road.

"We are regrouping at our command center base approximately seventy miles north of here. We will need approximately three days to regroup, and we will then advance upon the enemy. We have four companies defending the main interstate highway approximately twenty miles west of here, and two companies defending the other state road to the east of here. We are coordinating efforts with adjacent states to stop ISISA from advancing north. When the battle in the cities became fierce, we had all ships, private boats, and other vessels and planes leave the affected cities and go north. After evacuating major sections of the cities by airplanes, we had whatever was left fly north as well. The enemy did obtain control over some private planes at the smaller airports in the state.

"We need you to now pay attention to our following commands. These are not voluntary suggestions—they are commands under the martial law statutes. You must obey the commands or be arrested. If you resist, you will be shot."

At this point, fear filled the audience, and the villagers started murmuring.

Captain Mark ordered his men to fire a shot in the air to quiet the crowd. He stated, "We need your attention now. In addition to the three commands, I am asking for five hundred volunteers to assist us in defending the mountain pass. You do not have to let us know now. I want the volunteers to meet us at 0700 tomorrow. We will meet for further instructions here at the stage, weather permitting, or at the high school auditorium if it rains. Anyone not volunteering, the women, children, and elderly, you are herein ordered to pack up whatever belongings, papers, and possessions you can load up in any or all your vehicles and relocate north of the base. Anyone not having a vehicle may pack one bag each, and we will have buses available to transport you to safety. The first group will leave at noon tomorrow, and a caravan will leave every two and a half hours, or as modified, as we will post a schedule on the town's bulletin board. Or you can call the major's office. All residents shall leave this town within forty-eight hours from 0700 tomorrow.

"The second order is that all essential businesses, banks, stores remain open until tomorrow night at 2100 hours so that you may serve those leaving and those remaining. The volunteers and our military will commandeer any necessary provisions needed in the defense of the state. You may keep track of what is necessary and send the bill to the governor's office for reimbursement of your costs. Any price gouging will be dealt with severely and be considered a felony crime. We need to take care of our defense team first, then those leaving second.

"Lastly, I need you to look around. My troops are stationed at the perimeter of this assembly. I need all adults to show some form of ID before you leave. We will be listing the names and addresses of everyone here. We also need anyone of Mideastern descent or of the Muslim religion or who may have traveled to the Mideast or a Muslim nation in the past five years to go to the blue tent off to the right for special processing."

After that statement, the liberals started shouting at Captain Mark all kinds of obscenities and opposition. Captain Mark ordered one soldier to fire his rifle over the head of the assembled. Captain Mark had two soldiers point guns at the two leaders of the opposition, and they stopped shouting.

He said, "One more outburst and you will be arrested. I do not have to explain any of my orders, but I will tell you this: Four days ago, we were evacuating a town and a dozen Mideastern Muslims living or residing in the town commenced shooting at the assembled crowd and two hundred were killed and four hundred were wounded. We went to their homes and found information proving they were ISISA fighters planted for this planned uprising.

"We are not arresting or interning anyone unless we verify there is a threat. If they came into this country in the past eight years, we will check out all their background, where possible. Again, this is for your protection as well as the security of the state.

"Individual rights are suspended under martial law. Your mayor, police departments, all military reservists, National Guard, and state militia are now under my command. All reservists, National Guard members, or state militia personnel, as well as all former or retired military officers, are herein ordered to report to the yellow tent to my right and are officially ordered into active duty immediately. You are now under my command. You will have time to get your family off to safety and you are to report at 0600 with your family to leave before the first group.

"Any resident having only one son may leave with their entire family. Anyone who has more than one son, we ask that either you or any son over eighteen years of age and single volunteer to defend the village. Again, we cannot force anyone to volunteer, but if this village is not defended, ISISA will destroy the entire village. They are burning down all dwellings as they proceed north, so you will most likely not have any homes to come back to. All you must do is look to the south and see the smoke. They have destroyed most of the homes in the neighboring southern towns.

"The mountain road from the south is a good defensive position at the gap and could be defended by the five hundred volunteers for three days while the troops regroup up north for a counterattack and take over the fighting.

"So go home, talk with your family, help them pack whatever you may want. Businesses, please stay open until nine o'clock tonight and please open tomorrow morning at seven and remain open until told to close. All business owners, their managers, or their assistant managers, are to report to the green tent at the conclusion of this meeting to obtain instructions for their workforce. All employees of these businesses shall report to their employers immediately before going home for further instructions and/or assignments.

"No one can go south of the mountain pass. Armed troops are stationed at the bend in the road. No one can leave tonight, for the mountain road to the north has been secured until tomorrow morning, and no one may pass unless they are with a military escort. The lake region behind the park has also been secured by the military, preventing anyone to leave until tomorrow morning, and that is only with proper authorization.

"Anyone desiring such authorization needs to report to the police department at 0630 tomorrow. We request anyone owning a vessel large than eight feet long or any barges to also report to the police station at 0630 for further instruction. If you have any questions, please go to the brownish tent to the left and we will answer any appropriate question and direct you to what you need to do before tomorrow evening.

"We will demand your cooperation as you are now under martial law. Any resistance or rebellion will not be tolerated and will be dealt with swiftly. We have less than one week before ISISA breaks through the line of defense. They are in the villages less than sixty miles from here. We expect that most of our military forces will not make it and are willing to sacrifice this company for the benefit of this nation and particularly this state. If they are willing to defend this town, how many of you are willing to pay the price to defend your town? We will see tomorrow morning.

"So follow my instructions or go to the brownish tent if you do not know what to do. We have multiple handouts for each one of you. If you still have any questions, please see the mayor or the police chief at the police station in a half-hour, or Lieutenant Gilinsky in the brownish tent. This concludes the meeting. You are all dismissed."

The crowd was buzzing like a wild bunch of hornets. Some were downright indignant and very loud and complained to the mayor, police chief, or whatever official would listen to them. Then they went up to Captain Mark, shouting at him. He ordered his men to shoot them if they took another step. They were told to shut up, go home, and pack or they would be arrested or shot before morning. They were shocked and stopped. They looked at one another just as the armed men next to Captain Mark raised their guns and pointed it at them. Billy the Bully, who just happened to be the town's loud-mouthed liberal troublemaker, kept coming forward, swearing at

Captain Mark. The soldier shot him in the foot and told everyone the next shot would not be in the foot but either in the heart or the head.

Now everyone was terrified and the crowd became silent, and they began doing what they were told to do. They now realized the Army meant business and would not tolerate any more outrages. They took Billy to the hospital with armed guards and placed him under arrest. They bound him and placed duct tape over his mouth. His family was mortified because they were used to having their own way through their belligerence. This was different, and they became confused. The soldiers took their father away to the military prison located about seventy-five miles north of the village.

Several of our church group members went with Moe and Irene with the Bosnians to the assigned tent to assist them to get properly processed. They had been back to Bosnia three years earlier to visit their family members who had passed away and went to attend their funeral. Moe and Irene had gone with them three years earlier, so they, too, had to go and get processed. The church members vouched for them and their loyalty to the USA, and after an hour, they all were released after searching their home.

The members of our church who had previously been officers in the military, such as Captain Gary, Captain Roger, Colonel John, Major Eric, and a few others who served in the military as regular enlisted men, joined them and reported to the yellow tent. Captain Mark looked at these individuals, and Captain Roger, who was eighty-two years old and in a wheelchair, said, "Captain Roger reporting for duty." Colonel John, who was seventy-seven years old, and Captain Gary, who was sixty, both said the same thing. Captain Mark asked, "Who are these other men?" They each said who they were, but because they were not officers, he dismissed them and told them to come back tomorrow morning if they were under sixty years of age or younger. Captain Mark thanked them for their prior service and willingness to serve, but he was not running a senior day-care service.

Our church members gathered just before sunset, as we had done for the past seventy evenings. It now became noticeably clear in each of our minds what each of us was called to do. As we gathered, we started with songs of praise and worship, as we had done for the past seventy evenings. We had seventy-five members there. Some of us were a bit confused because the Lord had told us that seventy were called but we had seventy-five. What did this mean? After worship, Rabbi Maskil asked Irene if she had a word for the group. We prayed in tongues, and it was like the heavenly host was there, praising with us, and it was such an angelic sound that we were in awe. Within ten minutes, five of the members decided to pack their bags to leave in the morning because they lacked the ability to trust in God to conquer their fears. They cited family commitments had to come before defending this town. They left crying and disappointed in themselves.

Just then, Irene started to speak. "My children, my sons and daughters, I love you because you love and reverence My holy name and My Son, Jesus. Your prayers and concerns have reached My throne. I am the God who heals, Jehovah Jiro. For the next twelve days, all will be made whole. I will pour out My Spirit upon you and fill you with the courage, boldness, and strength you will need to 'stand your ground with confidence, peace, and joy.' So the military leadership, the mayor, and the rest of the town will know I have sent only you to defend this town. I will more than heal you spiritually, and so I am now healing all those who are sick. I am strengthening the limbs, the legs, the feet, the necks, the spines, the backs, and the arms of those here. The two of you who are crippled, arise now and walk. The damage due to the stoke on the left side shall be made totally whole, and all will function perfectly. I am adding the strength of Joshua when he was eighty to all those here. I am giving you the courage of David and Gideon to all the seventy chosen who will give their life for Me. I am pouring out My Spirit now to give you the boldness of Moses and the prophets when you confront those in authority or those who doubt you for My sake. So now, all be healed as I have spoken. Stand up, be healed, and be strengthened like you were when you were thirty years old. I am healing all your eyes and will grant you perfect vision. Even those who are blind or of poor sight will now see and see better than all the rest. Accept this gift I have for you and trust.

"After today's meeting, you have figured out that you are called to defend this village so that My name, Yahweh, will be known throughout this land again and in Israel again. All will be in awe of how I strengthened you and delivered you. My Name will go forth, and a new revival will break out within the year as the countless stories are told of how this town and eleven others were protected by My power, My strength, and My Spirit, and that the military had nothing to do with it. I have chosen the weak so they will know that it was not by power or might of this nation's armies that evil was defeated but by My Spirit, says the Lord of host. Therefore, go in peace and enjoy the evening. Rest and flex your muscles in the morning. I have restored the days of your youth for the next twelve days. You shall retain your newfound strength based upon the level of your faith and love for Me as well as your commitment to My instructions. Now go home, rest, and when you awaken, return once more for final instructions and My blessings."

As soon as Irene finished, Pastor Dave said to the congregation, "The Lord said He has now healed us and for us to arise and accept our healings. Roger, the Lord said your legs and your entire body are healed, so stand up and accept your blessing."

Roger looked at the pastor and said, "I have been crippled for nearly twenty years."

The pastor replied, "Yes. That is why the Lord wants to use you and has healed you. Everyone knows you as a cripple, so arise, increase your faith, and accept your healing."

Roger looked at the pastor and began to get out of his wheelchair. He noticed his left and right hands had movement and that he was getting full function and movement from his left side and his legs. He had no pain and took one step, smiled, and then a second, third, and he started to walk fast and then run and then jumped up and down. As soon as this happened, most of the people there started to notice they, too, were healed and getting strong. Pierre, who was blind, shouted out, "I can see! I can see! Praise the Lord." Those who had back, neck, leg, arm, or any other pain or disabilities were completely healed.

....

Our church group gathered at five in the morning before sunrise, the morning of the seventieth day. It was a beautiful Saturday morning, the first day of July. Today, everyone in town would have normally started preparing for the annual Fourth of July celebration in the park. We had been silent the past sixty-nine days as to what the Lord had in store for us. Outside our little village, chaos was the order of the day, but here in Bethel, there still was a sense of peace and tranquility in our church community. We gathered in the main church, as we had for the past seventy days.

We commenced with prayer and worship as usual for over thirty minutes, praising the Lord, beginning by singing "Praise Him in the Morning" and "Blessed Be the Tie That Binds." Then Rabbi Maskil looked at Irene and said, "Irene, I know you have a word for us." Then he looked at Estelle and said, "Estelle, I sense you, too, have a word for us also. Irene will go first, and then Estelle. Please get up when you are ready to deliver the Lord's message." We prayed in tongues for ten minutes, and Pastor Dave led us in two songs. We sang two more songs, "Here Is My Servant" and "The Call," both by John Polce.

After we finished the second song, Irene started to speak. "My faithful servants, you have been faithful for seventy days, and the big test of your faith and courage will occur during the next twelve days. Do you trust Me without borders or reservations? Do you have the faith of Abraham? Will your trust in Me to show the world your courage like no other? The courage of Gideon and his three hundred;

David, My servant, who defeated Goliath; Moses, who told the pharaoh to 'let My people go'; Joshua, who was eighty years old when he led the Israelites into the promised land. The courage of the prophets who were ridiculed by the kings and their courts when they were told about the king and the princes of their impending death and exile. You have already borne the scorn of the town for over ten years, and now the hour has arrived. You have prayed for many years for Me to use you mightily. Now, you must continue to focus upon Me and not the situation at hand. Just as Esther was chosen, you have been chosen for such a time as this. Abraham brought his son to be sacrificed on Mount Moriah, but My Son willingly went to be sacrificed for the world, a world full of sin and evil.

"I have chosen seventy of you to defend this most unworthy town. You will be alone. The villagers are so full of fear and selfishness that they will not volunteer. There will be a few who will appear to volunteer, but before the fighting occurs, they will desert their post. Some will leave as soon as the military and the last of the villagers leave this town. It is all for show. It is not for them that you will save this town but for My glory and so the world will know that I am with you and My Spirit saved this town. They will know the name of Yahweh and the name of My Son, Jesus. The Spirit, which lives in each one of you, will be with you for the next twelve days. So fear not, be of great courage, and execute the tasks that I have assigned. When the Army and the people return, they will know what you did in My name. They will see My glory written on the mountain.

"They will begin to believe that there is a God that protects. They will also see that I am the God that heals. All have been healed of their infirmities. Go to the meeting with authority. Go with your wheelchairs, canes, walkers, and when they reject you, show them I have healed you. Show them I have strengthened you and show them you have the strength to bend metal bars, something their strongest soldier cannot do. Tell them I have given you a plan to defend this town with only the seventy chosen by God.

"As for those I have chosen to lead, you must lead as My Son led, a servant leader. The leaders must wash the feet of those they are in custody of. You must not ask your assigned workers for anything for which you yourself would not do. You lead from the front like a Spartan king at the battle of Thermopolis. Each of them has a unique gift despite their apparent limitations. They, too, have been given a word, a piece of the plan. Just like a puzzle, just like the body, each has a specific function to fulfill so that everything works out for good. Listen to all, and you, leaders, must discern my truth and plan. For it is written, 'He who wishes to be great among you must be servant to all.' So, my servant leaders, do as My Son did, be willing to die for the flock, and sacrifice yourselves for the kingdom, for My glory and for the good of all the undeserving.

"You have your task to do, so arise at sunrise and I will have a final word for each one of you personally during the night in your dream, and I will remind each one of you of the task you must perform over the next ten days. Arise and review your notes to be sure all items are on the list in the order I have given them to you. The days of preparation will begin after sundown tomorrow. Present your list of needed items to the authorities or to the owners of the businesses. Do not accept a no from anyone. Speak with the authority of My Son. You will need to be bold and to stand your ground with the leaders of this village and the authorities. My Son spoke with authority, and now I bestow upon you My Spirit of authority to be bold in My name."

Rabbi Maskil interrupted. "Excuse me, I sense that Michelle has an important word because some are still fearful and have concerns. So, Michelle, please tell us what the Lord wants us to know."

Michelle arose and said to the church, "We need to sing one more prayer of worship. Let us sing 'For Those Tears I Died.'" After, Michelle said, "The Lord said to me, 'Be of good cheer and great courage. Fear not, for I will be with you over the next twelve days. "The battle is Mine," says the Lord. All you need to do is execute the plan I have placed in your hearts and minds. Be expeditious and execute the plan with great vigor and joy. Do not leave anything out because you do not understand the purpose. Just follow the instructions and you will overcome the evil that is about to come upon you. Mercy cannot be exercised in place of righteous justice. It is about what is in your heart.'"

She continued, "Some of you have concerns or questions about the commandment 'Thou shall not kill,' but I tell you that in the Hebrew language, the word or term *kill* means 'murder' and is very different from defending what is good or defending your family and friends. Do not murder but defend and follow the plan. Murder is of the heart, but to kill an evil person who is about to kill hundreds of innocent people is not murder. Most of the men coming here are very evil. They are the sons of Satan, the destroyer.

"Just as I led David and the Israelites in battle against the sons of Satan, so will I lead you against his new followers. You are not to attack but are to defend. Anyone passing the bend in the road on the other side of the mountain is fair game because they are bent on destroying you and the towns north of you. They are currently executing all whom they come into contact with, and they do so in the name of Satan, the destroyer. Also, do not rejoice over the death of these evil warriors. Rejoice only about the mercies and grace I have given you. Rejoice about being a good servant. Rejoice about My love and the fact that you have been chosen for the test."

Estelle spoke and said, "This is the Lord's final words for this morning: 'Go, My servants, to the park and present yourself as a group. When questioned, be bold and stand firm. Show them your youthful strength, bend the bars of iron, stand up, outrun their swiftest soldier. Tell them you have the plan and ask them for their assistance for the next three days to procure all that you need. I will put joy in your heart and peace in your activities. You will get stronger while the others grow faint. I know you will grow in faith and be strong with your perseverance to the task each has been assigned. When you become uncertain, talk to Me and I will send My Spirit to enlighten you and to direct your path. Now leave and stand your ground. Be of good courage, for I give you My peace."

Rabbi Maskil, Pastor Dave, and Father Jake said almost in unison, "We must now go. Go out with the gift that God gave you, the weapons God will provide. Do not fight on the terms the enemy wants you to fight. You must fight in the Spirit and with the plan your God has provided. We must go two by two into the ark, where God will protect us from all tribulation."

Just as we were ready to leave, Forshia said she, too, had a word for us. Rabbi Maskil told her to proceed. "My beloved, I know you are rejoicing for the miracles that just happened. Yes, be glad, so you will have completed the healing by the time you reach the park, even stronger, more alert, and more confident and at peace. I have extended much grace and mercy to all of you."

Pastor Dave gave us the benediction, and we sang three additional worship prayers. We sang "Glory, Glory, Glory" and "O Come Let Us Adore Him" and "Father, I Adore You." So we lined up two by two, with the pastors first, the musicians and singers next, the chosen leadership after them, and the rest of us. We arrived at the park at around six thirty-five. It was a beautiful day. So our group started to sing "Day by Day."

When we arrived near the park, Pastor Dave told us he needed to pray one more time and read from Philippians 4:6–8 and started saying, "Renounce worry, be not anxious, and overcome it through prayer. Lord, I need You. You are my one defense. Blessed is the man who believes in the Lord. God wants us to come to Him with our faith and our trust in Him. He is the God who protects and the God who saves. In the name of the Lord, we have the victory. Blessed be the name of the Lord. The name of the Lord is a strong tower, with the righteous running to it, and they are saved. Remember, Jesus is the center of it all, and everything revolves around Jesus and it is all about Him and not us."

The pastor told the men to put on a uniform, and the ladies were to wear the church's chorus robes. One-third would wear the red, one-third the white, and one-third the blue. Same with the pastors. The men who served in the military would wear the uniform they had previously served in. The rest would wear Army combat fatigues. Captain Roger had procured some uniforms from the Army-Navy surplus shop. In addition, all were to wear the red-white-and-blue scarf around their necks, and we were to wear our metal or wooden crosses on the outside of our garments. We all departed praising the Lord for all He had done for the entire church. As we departed to the park, we all started to sing "Oh, How I Love Jesus."

In the morning, at six o'clock, the mayor and Army captain gathered all the department heads in the town's park commons to go over the evacuation process of the town where the American armed forces were regrouping.

They had just received a communication from an Army scout that their company of soldiers sixty miles south had to fall back to regroup about forty miles from the village. They were also informed that some of their defenses were breached and they had lost almost half of their command. They would continue to try to slow down the advancement of ISISA until the military would be able to reinforce them.

They were informed where the fighting was. The enemy had over ten thousand troops in the region, and they were coming at them from three different directions. The fighting was fierce; they urged Captain Mark to expedite the reinforcement, with the recommendation that they needed another company immediately. In addition, they were also running low on ammunition and urgently requested to send some ammunition immediately.

When questioned about how he was to send ammunition and replacement troops to the military forty miles away, Captain Mark responded, "The general said it will not happen. We have extraordinarily little ammunition to spare until we get back to the base in the north. We will need the ammunition to defend this pass. They are brave soldiers, and they have been trained to handle it. They will fight to the last man. America will remember their valiant deeds." We stood in shark by the attitude of defenders being expendable.

Captain Mark told the mayor, town officials, and his officers that he was hoping for a minimum of three hundred volunteers, although he had asked for five hundred from the village, to remain as the second defense until the armed forces could regroup and return to combat the ISISA forces. He would see who would show up at 0700, to brief these volunteers. He said they might need to battle ISISA for approximately three days until the Army returned to take over the fight. Captain Mark asked the mayor, who was only twenty-six years old, if he would be one of the volunteers, but the mayor quickly responded that the people needed him for leadership in the refugee camp and he would be with the villagers at the refugee camp until after the fighting.

None of the department heads except for the public works director volunteered, and he stated that he would assist in setting up the defenses, but he left with the last crew heading north.

When we arrived at the park, we went up to Captain Mark, and Captain Roger, Captain Gary, Major Eric, and Colonel John got in front of him and said, "We are reporting for duty, and we have seventy volunteers to defend the town at the pass."

Captain Mark looked at the seventy and cried out, "Oh my god, is this all we have, a bunch from the geriatric ward, to defend this town against ten thousand young ISISA fighters? Sorry, but I will wait until 0700 to see how many of the village people will volunteer. I know your heart is there, but most of you can hardly walk without assistance. I saw you yesterday at the green tent."

The major said, "You think you Christians will be saved by your God! He is only in your mind!"

Rabbi quickly responded, "No, He is in our heart and our spirit. Christianity is not a spectator sport. There is a cost involved to be a player. True Christians are players who are required to pay the cost for the kingdom."

The mayor smirked while looking at the ladies in robes and said, "I get it, you're going to kill the enemy with your singing."

Pastor Dave responded, "Close, but no. We will use praise as a weapon! Praise God when all seems lost, and victory needs to be on our lips. When we praise the Lord, the victory will come."

When 0700 came, the mayor and captain said, "We will wait for another fifteen more minutes, and then we may just have to evaluate our options." Only ten other members of the town showed up. One of the selectmen, the public works director, a few men from the construction company and junkyard, and three others, all of whom were over fifty years old.

At 0730, the praise-and-worship team started to sing "Stand Up, Stand Up for Jesus." Then Colonel John, Captain Roger, Major Eric, and Captain Gary stepped forward and commented almost in unison, "We look at this as Operation Stand Your Ground. We may not move too fast, but you do not have to move at all when you are just standing your ground. Besides, we are all you have. God has healed us, strengthened us, and He has given us the plan for defending this unworthy town. We do not have to be fast, because God has given us a plan to hold this ground. Our strength is not in ourselves but in our mighty God. No one will get through the pass without killing all of us, and we are all prepared to die in service of the Lord Yahweh. Test anyone of us. We can do all things through Christ, who strengthens us."

After that, Captain Mark and the mayor kept mocking them a bit more. "We need fighting men. None of you are fit to fight, and you do not look like you're able to run. So what are the girls going to do, kill them with their singing? So who is this old guy in the wheelchair wearing Army pants, Air Force shirt, and a Navy hat? Is he confused?"

Colonel John immediately responded, "Captain Roger served initially in the Navy, then eight years in the Air Force, and finally sixteen years in the Army. He served three two-year tours of duty in Vietnam and was a helicopter pilot during those six years. As far as us running, these colors don't run. We will stand our ground to the last person." He pointed to the scarf, which looked like an American flag.

He continued, "The women are here as in the days of the Israelites, where the singers and musicians led the charge and called upon the name of the Lord to send His heavenly host to assist in the fighting. We will have strength in their songs of worship and praise. Our praises will become our weapons."

The mayor whispered to Captain Mark, and Captain Mark said, "Okay, we will test you. I want Captain Roger to run the one-hundred-yard dash against this twenty-year-old soldier, but he cannot use his wheelchair."

So Captain Roger said, "Sure, we accept your challenge. We also challenge you to pick a soldier to bend an iron bar and our sixty-year-old captain, Gary, will compete against him." The mayor told Captain Mark to accept the challenges, and he did.

Colonel John said, "Okay, if we win, you will allow us to defend this town, and if we lose, we will go on the next bus to the north. If we win both events under your terms, you will supply us a couple of dozen men to assist us to implement the plan that God gave us. Your men can leave at noon or sunset of the third day. Do we have a deal?" Then Captain Mark and the mayor laughingly said, "Sure, we have a deal." The mayor reassured Captain Mark that Captain Roger had been confined to a wheelchair for all the past six years in which he had been living in the village.

Pastor Dave and Rabbi Maskil told them that was the truth; however, the Lord last night healed all seventy and had made the cripple walk and gave all the seventy the strength of Samson. Pastor Dave said, "We stand by faith, not by sight, nor by feelings. Feelings are the devil's domain, but faith is God's domain. All things work together for those who believe. We make no excuses—excuses are a fake rationalization sprinkled with lies. In addition, about one-third of the men are seasoned soldiers who have fought in Vietnam, Iraq, and Afghanistan."

The mayor and Captain Mark laughed again and said, "Let the games begin!"

So we all went over to the track field about five hundred feet away. Moe went over to the finish line with three other members of the church, and they erected a cross about twenty feet past the finish line. Irene gathered the praise-and-worship team and instructed them to sing Sister Miriam Winter's song "God Gives His People Strength" and to start singing once the "Go" order was given.

Pastor Dave stood over Captain Roger and read Psalm 92 over him, which started with "Have you not heard…my strength shall be renewed." "Now, Roger, focus upon the cross and listen to the words of the songs."

Captain Roger arose from his wheelchair and took a few steps, which appeared to be a bit awkward. Pastor David jumped forward and touched Roger's legs and said, "In the name of Jesus, the Son of Yahweh, be healed completely. You are given God's heavenly speed, and may your footsteps be swift and strong."

They laughed again, as did the others who were watching.

Moe shouted out to Captain Roger, "Keep your eyes on the cross and not on the other runner! Run to Jesus!"

The ladies started to sing, "When He comes with a trumpet's sound, the weak made strong in the Savior's love, then My heart will sing, Jesus I am running to your arms." Captain Roger knew he was healed last night, but his faith was wavering a bit because although he was healed, that did not mean he could outrun this twenty-year-old soldier.

Now Captain Roger and the twenty-year-old soldier went to the starting line, and the mayor said, "On your mark…get set…and go!" The young soldier jumped to the lead, but as Captain Roger heard the words "God gives His people strength," he became confident in what the Lord had done—he not only surpassed the soldier but also made him look like he was standing still, just like in the *Forrest Gump* movie. The mayor, Captain Mark, and the soldiers stood there with their mouths wide open.

Then Captain Mark called a twenty-six-year-old monster of a soldier who was six feet, ten inches tall, and he must have weighed nearly three hundred pounds of pure muscle, to compete against five-foot, eight-inch Captain Gary. We asked for a crowbar, but there were not any available. Then Captain Mark had one of the soldiers get this three-inch piece of steel rebar off one of their trucks. Captain Mark's soldier could not bend it. The worship team began singing "There Is Power in the Blood." Then the soldier threw the bar at Captain Gary, and while they were still laughing again, Captain Gary bent the bar in half. Again, they were left with their mouths wide open. Captain Gary's wife, Michelle, asked the soldier to bend it back, and when he tried, he could not even budge it. Michelle took the bar away from the soldier, looked at the mayor, the soldier, and Captain Mark with a smirk, and then bent the bar back into its original position.

Then Captain Mark exclaimed, "I do not believe this! If I had not seen this with my own eyes, I would have said that this was impossible."

Michelle responded, "I can do all things in Christ, who strengthens me."

The worship team began singing "When the Saints Go Marching In" just as the rest of the seventy tossed away their canes and walkers and started to jump up and down in total victory and praising the Lord for all He did.

Colonel John told Captain Mark that he and the seventy would take the responsibility of the defense and presented to him the details of the plans God had given them over the past seventy days. He also stated that all we needed was a couple dozen strong young men and equipment for three days to help us prepare the defense. We needed access to several stores and facilities to get the materials we needed to defend the pass. Then they could leave at noon on the third day to join their families up north. He told him that they needed to evacuate the doubters within the next twenty-four hours.

We would need from the Army specific types of guns and ammunitions; whatever they could spare would be fine. Colonel John presented to Captain Mark the detailed plan that the Lord Himself had given to them. It was now 0800, and about ten others showed up to volunteer. Captain Mark said to us, "I want all of you to know that all of you will surely die, because if you can hold them off a couple of days, that will be remarkable. They will probably spend the next day burning down all your homes and the entire town. Those who are captured will be tortured brutally."

Moe replied, "Look around. We are all you have. You need not be worried. God's people do not cultivate hopelessness, as stated in Romans 6:10–16. You are not going to change your circumstances by worrying about them. Faith is trusting in God though it does not seem right. We trust in the Word of the Lord, and He will fight the battle for us, and we will obey what He told us to do. We are prepared to die a death of righteousness. We believe we have been given God's hedge of protection. We may be older, but we are wiser. Plus, God has given us an all-encompassing plan, and our trust is in the Lord our God and our strength comes from the Lord and not from our own strength or wisdom. Our faith is in the Lord and not upon the military returning on time. The people of this village have told you no way, but our faith and trust are in Yahweh and our Redeemer. The defense of this pass and the village has become our LOT—that is, listen, obey, trust."

Just then, Estelle broke out in song, with the rest of the team joining her. They sang, J. H. Sammi's song "Trust and Obey," followed by "To God Be the Glory."

Colonel John asked Captain Mark, "How many days do we need to defend this pass, and what can you give us to help prepare defend the pass?"

Captain Mark said, "Okay, okay, I get it. You are all mad, but I will review the plan. But our troops will need three days to regroup, so they will be back on the fourth day to relieve you, assuming some may live through this ordeal." He said he would give us fifty guns, ammunition, a couple of bazookas, two boxes of hand grenades, helmets, and jackets for our use. He would give us twenty or so soldiers of our choice based upon our needs. He would also order specific tradesmen to remain with the soldiers, but they would start leaving around noonish of the third day with the soldiers. We agreed. We also asked for the use of four helicopters to lift equipment and needed supplies to the top of the ridges. The worship team started to sing, "O Lord, for my reward is giving glory to You. Are you ready? Are you ready? Are you ready for God?"

Colonel John said to Captain Mark, "Here are the detailed plans, and we can review them now if you like!" as he presented several documents detailing each defensive positions. They gave us a key and the codes as well as several individual detailed drawings of each location, which were not drawn to scale but were very understandable. The drawings were marked as exhibits and were attached to the master plan.

Captain Mark and his top command staff stayed for over four hours, reviewing the plan and ordering some of his men to go with our appointed members of the seventy to procure the needed items. Plus, he called in the command center to send six heavy-duty helicopters. We told him we only needed four, but Captain Mark said, "You do not understand today's military. If you need four, you ask for six so that when they receive the request, they will send you only four."

Master Plan

SEE KEY TO PLANS

Key Index

Color Code	Meaning	Comments
	mountain peak	
	high mountainous area	
	rock ledge-verytical steep	
	rock ledge-gradual—not steep	
	rock ledge path, upper level	

●	cross	
	rock ledge path lower level	
	gravel embankment	
	staging area	
	path(s)	
	river	
	water	
	road way	
	drive way	
	rivine	
	defense positions	
	fake defense positions	
	door openings	
	entrances to george's and moe's facilities	

Codes To Numbered Containers

1. Observation deck built onto peek 20 x 40 for advanced lookout with telescopes and communcations equipment, small tent with mattress

1A. Observation deck built onto peek 40 x 60 for snyper/sharp shooter includes rifels with scopes, ammunition, rain gear, small tent, mattress

2. Slides/seesaw 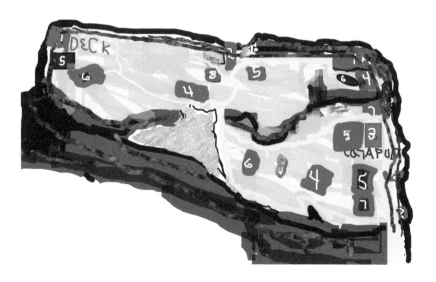 with rocks
3. Catepult with bobcat and fork-life equipmet
4. Ammunition in metal storage containers
5. Storage containers of barrel bombs, gas bombs, rock barrels with bobcat front end & folk-lifts near them
6. Large tent with camping equipment, grills, generator, lighting, communications
7. Large rubber slingshot for barrel bombs and gas bombs 3-10 gallons with fork-lifts and/or bobbact front end loader near them
8. Storage containers with barrel bombs—55 gallon only with fork-lift equipment
9. Large pile of 8" minus rocks
10. Storage trails with various equipment, supplies, bows, arrows, tools etc.

Defense Position Details

Defense Position 1
Second Bend—South Easterly Defense Position

Defense Position 2
First Bend & Southern Pass Defense

Defense Position 3—Command Central
George's Facility—Eastern Pass Defense

Defense Position 4
Moe And Irene's Facility—Western Pass Defense

Defense Position 5A
Southern Road Bend Defense

Defense Position 5b
Southern Pass Defense Position

Defense Position 5
Fake Defense Position—Wired To Explode

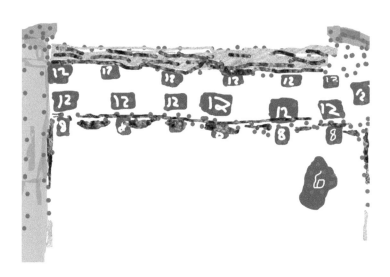

Defense Position 5c—Trust In The Lord
Northern Pass Defense—Stand Your Ground

Defense Position 6
Lookout—Swamp Defense Position

He looked intently at the plans and questioned the purpose for many different items, but we could explain all of them except the mirrors. We still did not fully understand the purpose of the mirrors and topliner, but we knew that the Lord would explain it latter.

Captain Mark, the mayor, and the others were no longer laughing. They were astonished, firstly, about the detailed plan to defend the town of Bethel and, secondly, how healthy and strong these mostly seventy-ish to eighty-ish individuals were. Their countenance of joy and peace changed knowing what they were about to do and that they would be overpowered by a far superior force that could easily exceed ten thousand fighters.

At noon, Captain Mark said, "These plans are so medieval, archaic, so like the A-team tactic, and so far out that it might just work because the enemy would never anticipate this multilevel, unconventional defense approach." He asked once again, "Who designed this plan?" and in unison, the seventy responded, "Our Lord and Savior gave us this entire plan!"

"When?" he asked.

Pastor Dave responded, "Over the past seventy days of prayer, fasting, and worship."

Rabbi Maskil also added, "Not by might, not by power, but by My Spirit, says the Lord. The battle is Mine, says the Lord of hosts."

Captain Gary's wife, Michelle, added, "We are not afraid. It is better for us to die being obedient to God's Word than to live with regrets. We will be going home one way or another. If we live, it is to be to our families, or if we die, we will be going home to our heavenly Father and our Lord and Savior, who will be waiting to greet us as good and faithful servants."

Captain Mark responded, "You people are crazy! I have never seen anything like this. I should be evacuating all of you, yet I need the three days for someone to hold back the thousands of ISISA troops in order to give us a chance to regroup into a cohesive fighting unit. Most of our crack troops and spare assets are committed to defending the main north-south route twenty miles to the west of here and to the east of here, and I cannot spare anyone to hold this pass. I need more than just you, and this village has no one else who has the courage to fight or make the needed sacrifice to hold this pass. What I am more astonished with is how yesterday I saw you as a bunch of feeble, weak, old people who portrayed yourselves as a bunch of religious kooks, but today I saw an eighty-year-old cripple outrun my fastest soldier, while a sixty-year-old man bent an iron bar that my strongest soldier could not budge, and then a sixty-year-old woman bent it back into shape. Your church group has something special going on here."

Rabbi Maskil responded, "Your opinions need to be adjusted by the truth. We are not fighting mortals; we are fighting principalities and demons. ISISA is not fighting us. They will be fighting the Lord's heavenly host. God's foolishness is wiser that man's wisdom."

Captain Mark responded, "For the past four hours, I reviewed the most resourceful, the most comprehensive defense plans ever conceived using little more than a bunch of junk. I look at the youth of this town as a bunch of cowards, yet your faith in your God, the trust without bounds, and the courage and fearlessness are like no other I have ever seen. May your God, whom you call Yahweh, and His Son, whom you call Jesus the Christ, the designer of this defense plan, continue to strength you, inspire you, and assist you in holding this pass. I will notify the command that we only have eighty individuals, that a plan has been designed to defend the pass, and that we have entitled this operation as Operation Stand Your Ground. I agree with one of the initial statements you made earlier this morning to the mayor when you first arrived, that being you were reporting for duty to defend this undeserving village. This was quite accurate when only ten others who were also over fifty years old stepped forward to make the ultimate sacrifice for their village. If you can hold this pass for the needed three days, this will go down in history like the Alamo, where three hundred held the position for a week against five thousand invaders."

Rabbi Maskil said, "We prefer to compare this with the three hundred of Gideon's men against the hundred thousand." Irene broke out in song, and the worship team began singing, "Lonesome Valley."

Father Jake, Pastor Dave, and Rabbi Maskil stepped forward and said to Captain Mark and the mayor, "We are not volunteering to save this village. We are volunteering to serve our God, our Lord and Savior, as His servants and out of love for Him because He asked us to. For He so loved the world that He gave His only Son. We are doing this for the glory of God so that the world will know that God does exist and that He can use a bunch of feeble old people to prove it. He can still make the cripple walk or run, the weak strong like Joshua or Samson, and the faint of heart with the courage of David and Gideon. It is so that the world will know that our God reigns and He loves all His people, even those who continue to ignore Him. He is calling them back so that when the days of the tribulation come, they may not be put to the test."

Captain Mark said to them, "I have seen movies about Samson but know nothing of Joshua, David, or Gideon. All I know is what I see. I see great wisdom, great strength, and great courage and eighty brave individuals willing to do the impossible for the ungrateful. May your God sustain you. I will get the helicopters and have my men assist you until we are ready to leave, when all the other villagers have been evacuated. I will issue vouchers to procure from the town whatever you need on your list. Give us a list if you need anything from the neighboring towns. May your God protect you as He has said." At that, Captain Mark ordered twenty-four of the soldiers with specific skills to assist them immediately. Moe, George, and Captain Roger provided lists of needed items to the captain. With the help of Captain Mark, the mayor, and the police chief, they were able to procure whatever we requested or needed.

They received a message from the command center that they were going to be sending four heavy-duty equipment-carrying helicopters, their strongest load-bearing helicopters, along with twelve soldiers with equipment and the specific skill sets needed in the preparation. Captain Roger was extremely happy because he wanted to fly again. He had been a helicopter pilot during his three tours in the Vietnam War, where he served when in active duty, and between tours, he flew C-130s from Guam to the bases in Vietnam.

That afternoon, we broke up into teams, and with the assistance of the Army and the twenty other volunteers, we brought the materials to the church staging area, awaiting the helicopters' arrival.

The preparation and setup teams and their duties consisted of the following:

Prayer and intercessory team: Father Jake (Catholic priest and charismatic filled with the Holy Spirit), Pastor Dave (Protestant pastor of a nondenominational church), Rabbi Maskil (Jewish rabbi), Irene (retired nurse and wife of Moe), Diane (Rick's wife), Estelle (Bob's wife), Michelle (teacher and wellness adviser), Anne (Pastor Dave's wife), Loren, Hailey (Michelle's daughter and an accountant), Pastor Forshia (Major Eric's wife), and Monique (Tom's wife) from the church.

Strategic defense coordinators: Colonel John (Vietnam vet and accountant), Captain Gary (Iraq vet and retired police officer), Moe (business strategist), Major Eric (former Air Force major and former VP of manufacturing), and they asked Captain Mark from the Army to work with them with his selected men.

Ordnance and explosive setup: Lieutenant Bernie (owner of a gravel pit, who processed sand and stone), along with six military personnel and two volunteers from his quarry.

Artillery and catapult setup: Vinko (carpenter and medieval-times buff), Jasmin (Bosnian and son of Niaz), plus two volunteers from the recreation department.

Construction of staging areas, barricades, and materials: Steve (owner of the construction company), Ralph (an engineer), Peter (distributor of construction materials and equipment parts), Carmelo, a.k.a. Carm (construction superintendent), Nick (construction superintendent), and two of Captain Mark's soldiers.

Barrel and propane setup: Harry (owner of the closed barrel manufacturing company), Lee (hardware store owner), plus three volunteers from the public works department, one volunteer from the gas station owned by George, and two volunteers who previously worked at the barrel company.

Communications, drones, and helicopter coordination: Captain Roger (three-time Vietnam vet, helicopter pilot), Josh (telecommunications and radio and cellular tower specialist), Charlie (CB buff and electronics store owner), Bob (a salesman), Gordon (former IT engineer).

Forest defense initiative: Lou (Vietnam vet who served as jungle fighter), Normand (also a Vietnam jungle fighter), six soldiers from the command, Thomas (a woodsman), Paul (a trapper), and Kyle (a fisherman).

Then the four mountaintop position setups and coordinators.

East mountain pass (home of George): George (gas station / variety store owner and former gun dealer before the guns were taken away), Larry (Marine sniper in Iraq), Richard (retired schoolteacher and football coach), Sko (retired school athletic director and football coach), Gene (former businessman and teacher), and Mike (sharpshooter during Vietnam).

West mountain pass (home of Moe and Irene): along with Moe were Jack (former Navy SEAL and sniper in Afghanistan and Iraq) and the Bosnians, Sajed (toolmaker), Ruffard (UPS driver), Humdia (toolmaker), Sade (toolmaker), Niaz (heavy equipment mechanic), and Sean (sharpshooter during Vietnam).

Southwesterly mountain surveillance and sniper position: Tim (Marine sniper in Iraq), Aaron (served in Afghanistan for Army intelligence and surveillance), and three soldiers.

Southeasterly mountain observatory and sniper position: Joel (former Navy SEAL and sniper in Afghanistan), Pierre (sharpshooter during Vietnam), Joe (sharpshooter during Vietnam), and three soldiers.

Mountain pass defense, debris, and barricades: Rick (construction laborer foreman and Marine who served in Vietnam who had a tattoo, "We the People"), Anthony (owner of the closed concrete plant), Henry (junkyard owner and former Army sergeant during the Vietnam War), two of Henry's employees (who were also members of the church), Jeremy, Larry, Sam, and Keith (the four were expert marksmen who served in Vietnam with Rick).

Medical supplies and food provisions: Rene (former Army medic during Vietnam War), Fran (Rene's wife and part Native American Indian), the five wives of the Bosnian men, Aboud (Lebanese hummus shop owner), and Jim (EMT paramedic and served in Vietnam as a medic).

All in all, there were seventy from the church, twenty-four soldiers from Captain Mark's command, twelve soldiers who came with the four helicopters, four helicopter pilots, twenty other volunteers who worked for the construction company, barrel company, or sand and gravel company, along with the ten volunteers from the town public works and recreation departments. All of these worked the plan under the command of Colonel John and Major Eric based upon the plan developed by God during the seventy days of the word.

Most of the materials were gathered were brought to the church property, with the property being adjacent to the northern side of the mountain pass. These are the main items that were brought there:

From the junkyard: a crane, junk cars, buses, engines, tow trucks, flatbeds, sheet metal, scrap metal.

From the construction company: Jersey barriers, bulldozers, front-end loaders, light towers, steel plates, steel beams, water buffalos, plastic explosives, caps, discharge boxes, dump trucks, gas-powered generators, solar-powered message boards, forklifts, Mantis cranes, storage trailers, storage containers, graders, concrete sewer pipes, compressors, metal water pipes, and rebar.

From the concrete plant: concrete blocks, Jersey barriers, concrete mixers, stone, sand, and other liquids.

From the quarry: sand, stone, riprap, boulders, dynamite, caps, wiring, front-end loaders, tractor trailers, and dump trucks.

From the closed barrel company: 1,400 barrels of various sizes ranging from fifty-five-gallon to five-gallon to coffee-can-size containers, barrel covers, machine parts, 2,400 hundred-pound boxes of ball bearings, aluminum and iron plates, and beams.

From the hardware store and the lumber yard: ball bearings, nuts, bolts, screws, mirrors, gray-blue tarps, brown tarps, black tarps, rope, wire, cable, various containers, lumber, axes, picks, grub hoes, and tools of various kinds.

From the variety store and gas station: gasoline, diesel, Blue Rhino propane tanks, refrigeration equipment, flashlights, oil, spare parts, rope, food products, red raw blood-dripping meat, coolers, and ice machine.

From the town's recreation department and highway: ten medieval catapults (both the spring-action and the slingshot type), ten slides, baseball bats, baseballs, tarps, canvas, fencing, javelins, bocce balls, croquet balls, baseballs, rope, hammers, disk and other sports balls, a Civil War cannon with twelve cannonballs and other round objects, two large whaling harpoons with six harpoons, dump trucks, flatbeds, metal garbage dumpsters of various sizes, storage trailers, compressed air tanks, fire extinguishers, oxygen and acetylene tanks, compressors, and all the pyrotechnic rockets and flares that were for the Fourth of July celebration.

From the technical shops: wiring, walkie-talkies, speakers, cell phones, drones, wiring, laptop computers, and monitors.

From the clothing and sports stores: mannequins and related body parts, jeans, camping gear, camouflage outfits, bows and arrows, fishing line and gear, knives, axes, and hatchets.

From the Army surplus shop: Army fatigues, gasoline storage tanks, knapsacks, blankets, various containers, water containers, fuel containers, bows, arrows, walkie-talkies, Army rank medals, leather jackets, uniforms, camping gear, clothing, footwear, and boots.

From the bowling alley: large and small bowling balls and duck pins.

From the Army: fifty automatic M16s and AR-15s, eight sniper rifles, eight bolt-action M1s, and eight shotguns and fifteen boxes of ammunitions for the automatic rifles, seven boxes for each of the other rifles, seven boxes of hand grenades, a bazooka with seventy rounds, and four flamethrowers fully equipped.

In addition, Captain Mark's soldiers commandeered two gasoline trucks with ten thousand gallons of fuel, and one oil truck containing six thousand gallons of fuel oil from the neighboring villages just north of our town. They brought them to the church staging area and surrounding fields.

During that afternoon, four platoons of soldiers escorted the villagers, including the mayor, the town's selectmen, and those in the hospital clinic to the designated refugee outpost set up for those evacuating the defense areas. Convoys of one hundred vehicles, trucks,

RVs, and trailers were escorted out one group at a time. During that afternoon, nearly one-third of the villagers departed under escort.

The rest of the villagers were systematically evacuated during the first two days, and the business owners and other volunteers were evacuated at 1500 on the third day.

On the eve of the three days of preparation, the seventy gathered together at sunset at the church. This time we were joined by the forty other volunteers who agreed to help in the preparation. We opened the meeting with prayer, song, praise, and worship for an hour and opened the worship portion with the songs "How Great Thou Art," "I Believe in You, the God of Miracles," "Our God Reigns," and "Lord, I Believe," followed by the American anthem and the Israel national anthem, and we concluded the praise section with "Thank You, Lord" and "Here Is My Servant."

After the praise and worship, Michelle stood up and spoke. "I sense the Lord is pleased with us today and with how bold we were to give Him the glory."

Just then, Irene got up and said, "The Lord, our God, the creator of the heavens, the earth, and all that have ever been created, says, 'I am pleased with what you have accomplished today and for your continued love, dedication, and response to My requests. You are My servants. The biggest tasks are still ahead during the next three days, and then the trials will begin. The foundation of our faith is not your tradition or religion. It is Yeshua Jesus and Yahweh.

"'Will you remember LOT? Will you still be faithful by continuing to trust in Me and the plan for your defense, or will you allow the evil one to fill you with fear, anger, and doubts? Will you fear and doubt when the Army fails to return in three or four days? Though you will walk through the valley of the shadow of death, will you fear no evil, though some fall at your right and some at your left? I will be with you through the next ten days. I am sorry to say that some of you will fall because you will not follow my plan but augment it with your own wisdom, and some will feel that their plan will be better than Mine. Some of you will fall for your disobedience but you will be with Me when you do. Some will make the sacrifice and fall to save others, and there is no greater sacrifice than to give one's life for another. Despite this, most will pass this test because they have kept their focus upon Me.

"'I have given you strength, increased your faith, made you bold, and instilled in you great love and great courage. I have told Michael to gather the host of angels and place them as protection over you during the next twelve days. Michael will assist the leadership to remind them of every *tittle* of the plan as I have instructed you to write down. When you hear the bullets whizzing by, do not fear. Just remember that the bullets have just been deflected by My angels. Do not be foolish, do not tempt the Lord, your God, for foolishness is not from Me. Be confident in Me but do not take unnecessary risks. When the battle begins, you should start praying, praising, and worshipping Me with your whole heart, mind, and soul. Sing loud and sing a new song unto the Lord of hosts. Follow My instructions about the songs and the order of the song and all will go well for you.

"'A few additional items to add to our plan: Move all the church speakers and equipment to the two mountain dwellings and broadcast from those locations. Let the enemy hear your songs of praise. This will upset them and drive them as if they were madmen. Place the flags of My beloved land along the pathways, along with the flags of the home of the brave. Wire every tenth flag with explosives. This, too, will infuriate them and make them like drunkards. Place My Son's cross at the bend, at the southerly portions of the two mountain dwellings along the pass. Place lights on them, and this, too, will drive them bonkers and commit them to do foolish acts. My beloved, go home, rest, and come here at sunrise for more instructions. I would also thank the other forty for joining us this evening as a witness of My faithful love.'"

Then Father Jake gave us his blessing, and Rabbi Maskil gave us the blessing from the Old Testament in which Aaron blessed the tribes of Israel. Pastor Dave arose, then he read Psalm 91 and spoke. "Trust in your training. Trust in God's plans and God's promises. During the heat of battle, pray from victory and not for victory."

Captain Mark and his soldiers, as well as the twenty volunteers, did not know what to make of these prophetic words. They were abuzz as they went back to their tents in the park.

That evening, after worship, Rick and his team began working with a portion of Henry's team to bring the junk cars, trucks, buses, and school buses to the church field so they could start placing them in the morning along the roadside after services.

THE THREE DAYS OF PREPARATION

On the first morning of the three days of preparation, the seventy gathered together at sunrise at the church, as we had done for the past seventy days. We opened the service with prayer, song, and praise and worship for an hour and opened the worship portion with the songs "What a Mighty God We Serve" and "Our God Reigns," followed by the American national anthem and the Israel national anthem and concluded the praise section with "Onward, Christian Soldiers" and "Mighty Fortress."

Irene got up and said, "The Lord, our God, says to follow the plan. Do not deviate from it or add to it other than what is listed by the leadership. Woe to he who adds his own will over that of the Lord. He said, 'I will give you two more hours of daylight each day for the next two days. I will renew your time and you will work in unison among the teams. I have appointed the leadership. Do not challenge them. Remember, the Israelites challenged Moses and I opened the earth and swallowed them up. Do not be foolish or prideful. Perform your task for them as if you were performing them for Me. Go, waste no time, and execute the plan that I have crafted for your defense and My glory.'" At that, we left the church and assembled in teams in the church field near the parking lot.

Captain Roger was a former Army pilot who flew helicopters and C-130 planes during the Vietnam War. He served three tours of duties, involving nearly seven years. He also spent eight years in the Air Force as an electronic technician and was familiar with the old-school technical techniques of radios, televisions, and electronic devices and operations of various flying devices. He was also a model plane builder and a drone operator. Every week he would fly his planes and drones in the park with Joshua and the kids. Captain Roger had owned the local tech store but had closed it four years earlier due to lack of funds for changing technologies and excess inventories that could not be sold. He lived in the rear portion of the store and had a stock of supplies that were considered obsolete and out of technology. He did some sales to maintain what he had previously sold, and he still dealt with some of the old-timers who did not like the new technology with all these chips that tracked everything one did.

Captain Roger had his team remove the loudspeakers from the park, the church, and Main Street, and they had them rewire the loudspeakers from the church to the two homes in the mountain and strung the wire along the sides of the mountain peaks for nearly two and a half miles with loudspeaker every one hundred feet and on the northern or eastern sides of the road nearly two hundred feet above the road. In addition, one speaker was placed every two hundred feet above the road along the narrow mountain path to the east, and the other on the western side about a hundred and twenty feet above the pass. Halfway between the speakers, they placed spotlights eighty feet above the speakers, and near the second defensive positions, dozens of strobe lights to distract the fighters. In the dark they looked as someone firing guns. So they placed additional mannequins dressed as soldiers approximately twenty feet above the lights.

Captain Roger also convinced one of the helicopter pilots to allow him to fly one of the units to bring the drilling materials to the mountainsides. He and the other pilots brought the twelve drilling units to the forty-foot level and the eighty-five-foot level, where there was a small pathway leading from George's home and additional units to Moe's homes to widen the staging areas.

The pathways were about fifteen to twenty-five feet wide, which would be enough to fit the equipment. The drilling crews from the quarry began drilling holes to place the dynamite or plastic explosives in the drilled holes. Each hole was drilled thirty-five to forty feet deep on the lower and upper levels and seventy feet in the upper levels.

They brought four Bobcat units to four locations on the top of the mountain and two larger bulldozers to the southern side of both George and Moe's home. They placed the very large 980G front-end loader along the roadway at three strategic places. They created a mini plateau at each of the other four locations. These became staging areas, and with the help of the volunteers from the construction company and the soldiers who were operating engineers, they leveled four areas near the top on the northern side of the peaks varying from six thousand square feet to twenty thousand square feet. They also created a plateau on the southern side of Moe's and George's home as a staging area for blasting a portion of that area. They cleared off nearly two acres of area using jackhammers, pneumatic hammer, bobcat, and bulldozers. These teams worked incredibly fast for two days to complete this task.

Lieutenant Bernie and his team, who worked at the quarry, took the drilling machines and blasting materials and commenced drilling holes on the east side of the mountain at the forty-foot level and again at the eighty-five-foot level about the roadway and on both sides of the mountain in the narrow mountain pathway leading into the town for an additional length of fifteen hundred feet up to the second bend in the road. They also drilled holes at the forty-five-foot and eighty-five-foot levels on the southern face of the western mountain for about twelve hundred feet.

They drilled sixteen hours a day for two days, and using the dynamite obtained from the quarry, the construction company, and the construction supply store, they placed it and the charges in the holes in order to blast away these forty-foot ledges. They wired the blasts into seven separate blasting sections. The wiring was covered up with clay, old leaves, or materials germane to the area so that it would not be seen or exposed to the weather.

Most of the sections were wired to George's home on the east mountain, but the two on the front west slope were wired to both George's and Moe's mountain home. The charges set at second bend and nearby and along the east mountain slope, the sixth defensive position, the first blast section on the other side of the bend in the road, and the charges laid in the sewer and drains were to be done electronically via Captain Roger's and Joshua's planes and drones.

Henry and Harry, along with their teams, started to fill the fifty-five-, thirty-five-, twenty-five-, fifteen-, and five-gallon barrels, as the Lord instructed. Some of the ladies worked on filling balloons with gas or kerosene and placed them in wooden boxes. They started to place nuts, bolts, screws, and ball bearing into the bottom third of the barrels, and then they began to fill the rest of the barrels with gasoline. When they ran out of gasoline from the tankers, they drained the gas of its fuel from the six tanks at the gas station (after they fueled all their vehicles). They capped the barrel tightly and aligned them in a row. Over the next two days, they filled up over 1,400 barrels with various metal objects and gasoline. They also filled up over 240 of the larger barrels with the fuel oil drained from the town's facilities. They filled another 700 barrels with 1-inch and 1.5-inch rocks. They filled five hundred coffee-can-size containers with both ball bearings, nuts, bolts, screws, and 3/8-, ½-, and 5/8-inch rocks and gasoline. The team sprayed all the propane containers (which were full) with orange paint, and the empty containers with navy-blue or black paint. They placed these barrels and the propane containers, which were full, into six groups for the helicopters and that crew to bring them to the designated areas. They placed the empty propane containers with the road crews. They also sprayed the various tanks of compressed air, oxygen, and acetylene, which were full of red or yellow paint, and they painted the empty tanks navy blue or black to distinguish them.

The town had a small zoo with animals from the area, which included wolves, foxes, wildcats, fisher cats, bobcats, moose, deer, and bears. According to the plan, we were to bring them to an area on the southern side of the mountain and release them in the forest next to the swamp. So Captain Mark called in a team of soldiers who took the animals and placed them in the personnel carriers and brought them upstream to the designated area using a barge supplied by the military. The military also had several Coast Guard gunboats blockading the river about thirty miles north of the town. Two of the deer got injured in the process, so Rabbi Maskil offered up this blood sacrifice to the Lord, as in the days of the Old Testament, so we sent the forest team to place blood-dripping meat along the forest path near the swamp, as designated in the plan. The team also set up charges at each end of the woods that could be electronically detonated remotely. This was to drive the wild animals toward the center of the woods when desired.

Rick was given a set of plans on how to line the roadway coming from the south. Starting at a point about four thousand five hundred feet from the southerly entrance of the pass, Rick's team lined both sides of the road with the vehicles from the junkyard. Using the vehicles that were damaged in the front and in the rear, they set them up so that they looked like there was a multiple-vehicle accident. This was done in order to gain the enemy's confidence to get them familiar, seeing the vehicles and other debris. No explosives were set on the first thousand feet of debris. Starting at three thousand feet, the team started placing empty barrels and empty propane tanks and American flags attached to the barrels. A hundred feet later, they mixed the American flag and the Israeli flags. The team had obtained over 400 American flags from the cemetery, which were placed there for Independence Day, and 170 Israeli flags also from the cemetery. In addition, Moe and Rabbi Maskil had purchased a few months earlier around a hundred Israeli flags from Christians United for Israel (CUFI) to celebrate the eightieth anniversary of their becoming a nation in 1947. Moe and Irene were also born in 1947 and said they "were born for a time as this," but they did not realize it until now what they were saying was somewhat prophetic.

On the mountainside of the road, we added other debris, such as car parts, pipes, engines, and scrap metal, from the junkyard and town dump. Every fifty feet starting at the thirty-five-hundred-foot level from the mountain pass, the ordnance team, led by Lieutenant Bernie, and six soldiers trained in setting explosive devices commenced placing barrels, Israeli flags, and empty propane tanks wired to hand grenades supplied by the military and plastic explosives supplied by the quarry. Rabbi Maskil knew that if the enemy saw the Israeli flag and attempted to pull it away to destroy it, it would pull the pin from the grenade, which was located beneath a barrel containing the gasoline and the ball bearings, screws, nuts, and bolts, whereby the impact of that explosion would send much of this metal flying toward the enemy, hitting, killing, or wounding quite a number of them. Crushed pea stone, 3/8-, 1/2-, and 5/8-inch stones were placed over the debris and the barrels to add a greater impact, and only the flags were above the stones.

As we came within five hundred feet of the first bend in the road, Lieutenant Bernie's team started placing the painted Blue Rhino tanks full of gas and the barrels with gasoline and ball bearings strategically along the roadside so that one of the snipers would be able to shoot it, causing a great explosion. By placing other small parts and objects above or on the tanks or barrels, a great impact of destruction would occur. The orange-spayed propane tanks and the yellow barrels identified which tanks were full. This effort was coordinated with assigned sniper units and some of the expert sharpshooters and marksmen. They would be directed from command center as to which barrels or tanks to shoot at due to a coding and numbering schematic developed by Colonel John.

As Rick's team reached the bend in the road, Vinko's team had dismantled four of the food booths set up in the park and reassembled it just before the cliff at the bend in the road. Rick's team unfastened the guardrails for nearly four thousand feet on the cliffside, commencing from the mountain pass, and used them in the pass defensive positions. They brought in sandbags full of pillows to make them look like they had sand in them and placed them in the front of the booths.

We placed several small American flags along the side, with an exceptionally large American flag and a large Israeli flag above the booth, covering or obscuring the view behind the booth. Behind the boots, they had relocated a large billboard that was placed high above, further obscuring the cliff behind it. We placed mannequins with damaged bolt-action guns behind the sandbags (which was filled with Styrofoam) and standing in and in front of the booth to look like a checkpoint manned with soldiers. According to God's Word revealed to one of the ladies, we anticipated the enemy would attempt to ram this checkpoint with the first wave of fighters.

Two other teams placed two hundred mannequins dressed in combat fatigues and plastic helmets along the first and second levels as well as at the mountaintops about two hundred feet above our defensive positions with toy guns for over two thousand feet between the second bend and the first bend in the road. They were positioned twenty feet just above the strobe lights, which was eighty feet above the spotlights and the sound system loudspeakers.

Henry's team placed a functional older bus near the bend on the mountainside, which a welder fastened steel plates to after they removed the seats on the left side of the bus. The plates were two half-inch-thick steel plates with slots to shoot from that were cut into the steel near the joints. There were five slots for five positions. Next to the bus, we placed a bulldozer, a 980G front-end loader with a five-yard bucket, and behind that was a tow truck with a crane.

The team placed six barrels with gasoline and ball bearings just after the bend and also placed the barrels on a sandpile with small rocks on top of them, completely covering them on the south side but leaving the base of the barrel exposed on the north side so that the snipers would see the orange to hit it and explode the barrels when instructed. The roadway was approximately forty-five feet wide, plus each shoulder was an additional twenty-five feet wide. By their placing the debris alongside the road, this narrowed the road. Twenty feet after the bend in the road, we stepped up the number of marked barrels, propane tanks, and flags wired with explosives because we expected the bulk of the battles would be fought in the area from the bend in the road to the mountain pass.

Rick's team placed the cannon at the northerly face of the pass along with two catapult units. He also placed two harpoon guns approximately one hundred feet apart. At the southerly position of the mountain pass, they placed two of the catapults. The other two catapults were placed at the east and west mountain command centers on each side of the mountain road at their southerly location. They also strategically placed many storage containers that would serve as protection for supplies, personnel, and the two catapult operators.

Lieutenant Bernie's team also strategically placed quite a few barrels, plastic explosive, and dynamite under nearly half of the sewer covers and drainpipes just before and after the two bends in the road up to approximately one thousand feet before the pass.

The drilling crews were also sent to the bends. They drilled down ten to twenty feet and placed explosives to blow away the road at the appropriate time. The devices were set to explode remotely via a telephone call from an attached cell phone or from another device that would be generated from one of the drones or model airplanes controlled by Captain Roger, Joshua, and their crews.

Colonel John, Major Eric, and their team inspected everything that was done and compared them to the Lord's plan for accuracy. A few changes had to be made due to omissions or changes the soldiers made, but the colonel had them adjusted back to the plan.

During the first two days of preparation, sunset was at ten forty-five instead of around eight forty. The Lord added two more hours of sunlight so we could complete our tasks. On the third day of preparation, sunset was at eight thirty-three.

One the morning of the third day of preparation, Steve and Rick's teams, along with other available personnel, moved the Jersey barriers, concrete blocks, water and cut-down sewer pipes, sand, and stone to three strategic positions along the road, as noted in the plan.

The first line of defense of the roadway consisted of Jersey barriers placed halfway between the mouth of the southerly portion of the pass and the first bend, where the fake checkpoint was situated. Behind each of the three defense lines were construction storage trailers. They placed three together, whereby the first two that were fitted with reinforced steel plates on the exterior walls would block any bullets or mortar fire from damaging the one holding the stored materials, guns, ammunition, barrels, and tanks. In addition, on the first two lines, Rick's and Henry's teams placed metal garbage trash bins, and we filled them up with sand and placed them in the center portion of the road. Each line of defense had seven of these metal bins. The metal bins would absorb bullets and propelled grenade blasts. The Jersey barriers were placed on top of these in the roadway. Steel plates, sand, stones, and other barriers were placed between each set of Jersey barriers, and concrete blocks also, to absorb the bullets and the blasts. Our defense barriers were ten feet high. Plywood and planks on concrete planks enabled us to walk on top of the bins to man our posts. Explosives and barrel bombs were wired to the next defensive position, so when one was escaping to the next position, the last man was to trigger the explosives.

The second line of defense with the barriers was at the mouth of the southerly side of the pass, and the final defense barriers were set near the mouth of the northerly side of the pass. These barriers were set after all work was completed outside of the first bend. All the guardrails were removed from the first bend to the northerly mouth of the pass. The railings were first placed to support the defense walkways to support the planks, and the excess were transported to the top of the four outposts.

On the entire width of the road and both shoulders on the mountainside and the cliffside, Jersey barriers were set up in layers four deep, and each layer from the front to the rear was elevated by two feet, except for the outer layer, which was the same height but looked like a double wall with three feet of sand poured between the layers and barriers resting upon the sand. Concrete was poured six inches on top of the sand to hold another layer of barriers. Six feet of sand and claylike pond fill was mounded in front of this outer layer, hiding the fact that Jersey barriers were in place. Sandbags were placed on top of the rim of the Jersey barriers to form a bunker. Four three-foot concrete water pipes were placed in front of the barriers, forming a funnel effect with two on each side of the road. Between the front layers and the middle and back layers were sand and stone to elevate the position in such a way that the defenders could easily shoot over the front defensive wall created with the barriers. The soldiers sent plastic explosives underneath the sand, which could be triggered remotely by a device to be located at George's home outpost should this first line of defense be breached.

There were openings in the rear of the defense on the mountainside so that the defense personnel could escape during a full-fledged assault and come back to the mountain path. A tunnel was created from this first defense location to the mouth of the pass using six- or eight-foot sewer pipes, with stone and sand piled above it, and dynamite charges to be placed at two locations to blow the pipes up after they retreated to the next mountain pass defense. Cars, motors, and other car parts were placed above and in front of these pipes to obscure the passageway.

In addition, there was an opening created at the top of the concrete so that as they might retreat from their defense, they could cut the plastic with a knife (that was taped to the concrete) holding the sand back. This would fill the central portion of the pipe to prevent the enemy from advancing through the pipe, causing a delay, which would enable the men to retreat. Once the last man passed through the tunnel, he was to flip a lever and trigger three explosions in the tunnel and a massive explosion blowing up the entire defensive position, junk vehicles, and containers they were leaving. Explosives were set about two hundred feet from the switch just after where the sand dropped in, one in the middle of the other side of the sandpile and one at the entrance of this tunnel, thus wiping out everyone in the tunnel and near the entrance. In addition, the detonation would also blow up six barrels containing fuel and ball bearings and other metal objects between the last row and the second row of the defense barriers.

The second level of defense was at the southerly mouth of the pass. The mountain pass defense was set up very similar to this first line of defense, except there were three water pipes on each stacked in a triangular fashion with a sewer pipe filled with sand in front of them to form a defense. Sand was placed in between the sewer pipe and the water pipes protecting the water pipes. The purpose of the two lower water pipes was to have a marksman and expert shooter take down the advancing troops as they advanced, yet they would be protected. They were to shoot only at the enemy in their direct line of fire, and they were provided with three guns each and an assistant from the service team when needed to reload their weapons. The back portions of the sewer or water forms for the first three feet were cut to prevent ricochets from occurring.

Also, this second defensive position had an opening created at the top of the concrete pipes so that as they might retreat from their defense, they could cut the plastic with a knife (that was taped to the concrete) holding the sand back. This would fill the central portion of the pipe to prevent the enemy from advancing through the pipe. During the delay, which would enable the men to retreat, once the last man passed through the tunnel, he was to flip a lever and trigger three explosions in the tunnel—one opening about two hundred feet from the switch, another opening in the middle, and one at the entrance of the tunnel—thus wiping out everyone in the tunnel and near the entrance. In addition, the detonation would also blow up six barrels containing fuel and ball bearings between the last row, storage containers, junk vehicles, supplies not used, rock piles, and the entire second row of the defense barriers. The blasts were set so as to send all the debris in a southerly direction.

The second and the final lines of defense also had two wooden catapults placed into position, a 150-foot metal storehouse encased in steel plates at the southern side relocated from the town's highway department, 150 barrels of various sizes filed with gasoline, and various metals (ball bearings, screws, wedges, nuts, bolts) and barrels filled with only rocks, riprap, or eight-inch-minus-size stones.

Just like the first pass defense, six- or eight-foot concrete pipes formed an escape route leading to the third and final defensive position. It, too, was wired and set up in a similar fashion. The entrance was through one of the metal storage buildings, and the pipe was covered with stone and sand initially, and then with buses, cars, and other debris from the junkyard to hide the escape route from view. Jersey barriers, concrete blocks, sand, and other materials were set up at the mouth like the first defense barrier for the entire width of the pass's mouth.

At both sides of the pass were sewer and water pipes arranged in a broken reverse V setup for the sharpshooters' post on the inside pipe, and the other pipes were filled with sand and the outside of the other pipes were covered with sand and gravel so as to obscure or hide the pipes. Two catapults were placed behind the storage barricades and storage sheds, with one near the metal shed, which contained the gasoline-filled barrels. The containers on the southerly side were fitted with the steel sheeting to protect the northerly sectors.

Along the entire perimeter and sides of the mountain pass, the drilling crews had drilled into the rock at the forty-five-foot and the eighty-five-foot levels above the pass to blast away the rock. Again, they placed explosives in the sewer and the water drainage pipes to be remotely controlled in part, and some were wired to devices located in George's home.

Tom's team placed at the mouth of the mountain passes to the south and to the north a one-hundred-foot American flag draped across the road about ten feet above the barricades, tied into the mountainsides. This also helped obscure the next defensive position.

On the entire length of the mountain pass were floodlights that could turn night into day for the crew manning the second defensive position. Also set up at these locations were light towers from the construction company, facing toward the first line of defense. Solar-powered and gas-operated light towers were also placed ninety feet above the pass at both George's mountain home and Moe's mountain home on the southerly front and the inside of the pass. They were protected by steel plates and set up behind rock formations with aluminum reflectors magnifying the light. They were also set up behind the pathway defenses and in the areas where the catapults were stationed.

The third and last level of defense of the roadway was at the northerly entrance of the pass. This defensive position was set up like the second line of defense. There were no sewer pipes to escape from. This final defense was where the team was to stand their ground. This was where the final battle was to be fought, and no one was to retreat. It was a fight to the death, fight unto victory, or fight until the Lord showed up, whatever was the Lord's will. Monique placed a large sign attached to the last northerly storage bin, which read, "Fear not, stand your ground," just in case some became weakened.

At each of the three defensive positions in the pass and road, they had storage containers to protect the materials from the bullets, and in front of the containers were mounds of sand and sandbags to further protect the ammunitions and barrels. The enemy had propelled rockets and mortar launchers, so we had to protect our supplies.

We placed a thirty-foot large cross in the center of this third defense line, George's and at Irene's home position, with a large

American flag on its right and a large Israeli flag on its left side. The cross was adorned with bright white Christmas lights, and one of the ladies placed a sign over each cross entitled, "Our God Reigns," in green, fluorescent paint, which could be seen for a thousand feet. We also set up two additional wooden crosses at the southerly side of each of the mountain pass homes owned by George and Irene. We attached lights so that the crosses would be seen during the night.

The barrels that were loaded with gasoline, ball bearings, screws, and other items were distributed to positions 1 through 5, with position 5 given half of the remaining barrels and positions 3 and 4 given 35 percent of the remaining barrels. Positions 1 and 6 were given 50 percent of the remaining barrels of oil, and positions 3 and 4 given the other half equally. Some of the smaller coffee-size cans were filled with marbles and picture frame wedges.

Positions 2, 6, and 5b and 5c received the pyrotechnics, where position 5 received sixty-five percent of that item. Positions 3 and 4 received other fireworks items like firecrackers, sparklers, blockbusters, and cherry bombs attached to wine bottles filled with gasoline and metal items.

On the morning of the third day, each team had to organize their defensive positions based upon the design and list provided by the Lord and summarized by the central leadership under Colonel John and Captain Gary. Rick's team had multiple defensive positions, and he was assisted by any available members, the military, or from the other teams. Tom was responsible for the northerly and southerly positions of the roadway pass, and Rick handled the first and second roadway positions. Everything at the bend in the road and the initial two positions was set to go, as well as everything between the bends. These positions were coded bend 1 for the first bend in the road, MRP-5A for the position halfway from the bend to the southerly mountain pass, and MRP-5B for the southerly mouth of the pass. The final position needing to be addressed by Rick's team, headed by Tom, was coded MRP-5C but also nicknamed MRP-SYG. At MRP-SYG, the team needed to close the barriers and bring in the remainder of the arsenal.

The teams brought in the cannon power, cannonballs, other round objects, the 320 coffee cans filled with ball bearings, screws, picture frame wedges for the Civil War cannon. They placed the various-size barrels filled with gasoline and ball bearings and other objects noted above next to one of the catapults behind three layers of concrete blocks and eight-inch-minus rocks, one- and two-inch granite rocks, and bowling balls and other round objects, full and empty propane tanks piled next to the other catapult, with two Bobcats and fuel for the equipment. The propane tanks were painted orange or yellow if they were filled, and blue or green if they were empty, so that the snipers would shoot at the full tanks when they were ten to fifteen feet above the ground, causing an explosion to injure the enemy. Some of the public works team members went around to the homes and took all the gas tanks from the grills left outside and brought them to the staging areas.

They created bunkers with sandbags, concrete blocks, Jersey barriers, sand, and gravel and also had steel storage sheds loaded with various lighting equipment, pyrotechnics, ammunition, a bazooka and additional guns, three crossbows with five hundred arrows, three regular bows with seven hundred arrows, hand grenades, and other items needed in the defense according to the plan.

Each of Rick's defensive positions was rigged to explode upon evacuating that position, to drop back to the next position. When the position was being overrun by the enemy, they would blow it up, destroying everyone in that position. Halfway between the pass, Tom and Rick created a fake defensive position wired to George's home. This fake position would give the teams retreating from the second defensive position enough coverage to get to the final defensive position. It would be extremely important for the defensemen to follow instruction when the order was given to fall back. Each person had to do their part with precision; otherwise, it would endanger the life of the remainder of the defense personnel at that position.

This fake defensive position area was booby-trapped. Mannequins were dressed as fighters with uniforms, old World War I rifle, and helmets. The mannequins contained three- and five-gallon plastic water bottles filled with gasoline, ball bearings, screws, and other small metal objects so that when the soldier overran the position and shot the mannequins, they would explode, eliminating a few enemy soldiers. Also, the mannequins were wired to explode once the enemy moved them or when command center detonated the entire area once enough enemy troops overran the position. The containers were wired to explode when the doors were to be opened.

Captain Roger and Josh had their team wire the sound system to all the loudspeakers, the security cameras, the communications stations, and the detonation devices to the adjoining room. They took an old music soundboard with five hundred switches, coded each position, and wired them to the specific locations for detonation. There were over eighty security cameras as far away as one mile from surveillance position 1. These security cameras were also positioned on various mountain location from positions at a thousand feet past the second bend to nine hundred feet west of the western lookout post. Captain Roger also mounted twelve security cameras onto his drones and model planes, which, like the other devices, could be controlled and viewed by the monitors set up at command center by Gordon. The volunteers, under the direction of Joshua, placed the floodlights intermittently between where they placed the speakers near the mountain peaks. The lights were protected with plexiglass and with aluminum metal sheets (which also acted as a reflector) in a visor shape and with rocks at the lower level. The same was done along the path, the first bend, George and Moe's defensive positions.

There were over sixty monitors, and most monitors had split-screen capabilities. They placed six of the security cameras in the woods and in the swamp area camouflaged in the trees using stuffed owls found at the zoo and fake rocks. The loudspeakers were also wired back to command center, but these were wired to the gathering room, where many microphones and several sound systems were brought in from the church, park, and town boulevard. They were tested out by Captain Roger and Joshua's team, and they were very loud, especially in the mountain locations. The loudspeakers were also concealed behind cleverly placed rocks, fallen trees, and tree stumps, and they were also protected against the rain by plastic coverings. We could hear the music and the singing clearly for over two and a half miles.

After the soldiers and other temporary volunteers left at around three thirty in the afternoon on the third day of preparation, the so-called ten volunteers who were to assist us in defending the pass left a half-hour later and took off in their vehicles parked at the church lot, but Fran saw them leave from the church window and reported back to Colonel John. This event had been foretold by a word of knowledge spoken by Irene during the seventy days, which foretold that the ten volunteers would pretend to stay but would leave before the fighting started once they felt no one from the village would see them leave.

The seventy knew it was only going to be the church members to defend the town, and it was not a big thing for them; they did not count on these volunteers, because their trust was in the Lord's promise.

Knowing we did not have enough guns and ammunition for all the fighters and the lookout posts, Moe and Colonel John called the rest of the seventy to George's defense-position mountain home to review the defense plans. Colonel John, Major Eric, Captain Gary, Lieutenant Bernie and Moe had been keeping track of the plans and inventory according to the Lord's plans, and they indicated that we were short guns and ammunition. We were also missing certain other supplies and items. Colonel John and Moe provided copies of all the missing items so that the seventy could look around the town to obtain the needed items according to the plan. We gathered at George's home, which now became command center. George had a large room where we were to gather for the next ten days. We brought in some of the tables, the benches, the cross, and the podium from the church into this room.

George asked what we were missing, and as we were handing him the list, Captain Gary told him that we needed another twenty-five fully automatic weapons with seventy-five clips and fifty boxes of ammunition for those automatic weapons, eight pairs of binoculars, four more sniper rifles with scopes plus scopes for the rifles that the Army had provided without the scopes, four boxes of hand grenades, six sets of bows and arrows, and forty helmets. We were only able to get twenty helmets from WWII from the Army surplus store.

George smiled with that big Cheshire cat's grin and said to us, "Please follow me." We went down a stairway in his mountain home to a room set up like a study, with a television, desk, and bookcases. George went over to the central bookcase and pulled out one of the books, which contained a key, which he then used to unlock something on the other bookcase, then pushed the bookcase in slightly and rolled it to the right. There was another, very large room lined with guns, ammunition, binoculars, helmets, bows and arrows, hand grenades, mortar rounds, equipment, and much, much more. We had forgotten that George had owned a gun shop that he closed six years earlier when the government took away the nation's guns. George had everything we needed plus additional gunpowder for the cannon, which would enable us to make our own bullets should we run out. Tom knew how to make the bullets and guns. He also had equipment and metal pipes to make additional guns. George also had the equipment, the lead, and the casings to make bullets.

While Colonel John, Captain Gary, Major Eric, and Moe stayed with George to take inventory of the items in the concealed room and to arrange to distribute the needed items for the six defensive positions and two outlook posts, the rest of the group were sent onto a scavenger hunt to obtain the other provisions needed.

After the group returned, we went over the assignments and who was to oversee the team at each location. We needed to have a chain of command so that each member and command center would know the positions or locations they were to be stationed. Within each defensive position, we created a hierarchy within the group with specific assigned task according to the plan.

The individuals identified were selected during the seventy days God had instructed via the words of knowledge given by Irene, Estelle, Michelle, and Rabbi Maskil.

The assignments were as follows.
First defensive position: outlook post, southeast (code word: OP-1).

This position was also known as the second-bend defense out-look position. From this position one could see for six miles down the valley toward the next lake village. Looking west, one could see to the next bend, known as position 2.

This location was the most southeasterly position, and they were to just observe enemy movement coming from the southeast. They were located at the point of the second bend in the road east-south-east of the first bend. This position was about two hundred feet above where our snipers or sharpshooters would be stationed during the battle. After reporting the enemy's location, the upper lookout would rejoin the other fighters at the defensive position located two hundred feet below.

Also, we set up the snipers with a high-powered sniper rifle on the west face of this position about three hundred feet above the roadway so they could see and shoot any barrel or tank from the westerly side of its position.

OP-1 was under the command of Aaron, who served in Afghanistan as a Marine in its intelligence and surveillance group, and he was an expert marksman. With him was Tim, a well-dec-orated Marine sniper who served in Iraq, and Charlie, who was involved with communications and was a CB buff and electronics store owner, as his team. Charlie was also a skeet shooter enthusiast and regional champ, and his initial post was at the upper level facing southeast, and once he submitted the intelligence to headquarters, he would join his fellow fights at the lower-level platform.

Although this team was a small team, their primary object was mainly surveillance up until when all the fighters past this defensive position and headed toward position 2. Their secondary mission was to stop the fighters from retreating past this position and for the snipers to shoot the barrel bombs and gas containers in conjunction with this mission. They were also to shoot at the barrel bombs being lobbed in the air by the catapults from positions 2, 3, and 5.

This position was an outcropping from the mountain with a lower defense area two hundred feet below so that two vantage points were available. One looking south and east and the other looking south and west.

Second defensive position: southeasterly mountain sniper position (code word: MSP-02).

This position was located just west of position 1 and 180 feet above the first bend in the road. It was fully equipped as a defensive position guarding the southwesterly and the easterly face of the mountain, which could be climbed and assaulted by the enemy. It also had a great view to the east and the west that would enable them to see the strength of the enemy coming from the south heading up to the roadway from the lake region. The soldiers and Lieutenant Bernie's quarry team were able to cut a path into the rocks about twenty-five to thirty feet wide and up to five feet deep connecting position 2 with position 3. This enabled the teams from each of these two positions to back up one another whenever needed. They also place rocks, sheeting, sandbags, and other protective objects on top of the walls leading between the position and George's upper path location.

MSP-02 was under the command of Pierre, formerly a sharpshooter during the Vietnam War. The other members of his team were Jim, a former Navy SEAL and sniper in Afghanistan; Sean, a sharpshooter during the Vietnam War; Joe, a sharpshooter during the Vietnam War; Kyle, a fisherman; and Mike, also a sharpshooter during the Vietnam War. Their primary mission was to guard the area toward the east and the bend, and they would be backed up by members from position 3. The position had much defense items, including barrel bombs, barrels filled with gasoline, gas containers, barrels filled with rocks, piles of riprap rocks, an old concrete truck, a bulldozer, a catapult, a front-end loader, mounds of crushed stones, two tents, twelve storage of containers, and many were filled with weapons, ammunitions, supplies, and provisions. Others were to protect the supply containers, and they had steel sheeting inside the containers and rocks and sand outside the containers.

This position was to be involved in all the major battles and required much protection from the area below. A wall of larger stones was placed as protection, which could be pushed by the bulldozer or the front-end loader.

Third defensive position: eastern mountain command center (code word: EMC-03).

As we looked from Moe's ledge, we saw the height of the mountains above George's home. At the third level was George's home, and beyond was the second defensive position.

When we looked below the upper portion of the range, we saw several stairs-like outcroppings at each level. Three levels of outcroppings with the lower two levels being twelve to twenty-five feet in width. The upper third level had a larger outcropping and a larger flat area for staging.

This position extended along the mountain to position 2 and went the entire length of the mountain pass. This position was the home of George, which was carved into the mountain and had a great 270-degree view of the southeastern mountain pass and the northern village. The home had six thousand square feet of living space and two thousand square feet of storage plus the garage plus that hidden gun room.

During the preparation period, they excavated and created a platform on both the southerly and western side of that mountain, creating a platform of seventy-five feet in a shape of a 7, which would enable them to defend a frontal assault as well as assist in the defense of the mountain pass. This position was now command center. There were three entrances from the home on the south, north, and west side of the home.

Strategic defense coordinators included Colonel John as commanding the entire defense effort for all positions. Assisting him was Major Eric, a former Air Force Major and former VP of manufacturing, who coordinated the defense of the EMC-03 position;

while Lieutenant Bernie, the owner of a gravel pit and processed sand and stone, coordinated the detonation of the wired explosives, and Captain Roger, a helicopter pilot in Vietnam, and Joshua, a telecommunications and radio and cellular tower specialist and drone enthusiast, were in charge of communications, drones, and motorized model airplanes. Also assisting them was Gordon, a former IT engineer, who was primarily assigned to monitor the surveillance equipment and communicate the activity to Colonel John and Major Eric.

The pastors, rabbi, and the worship team, comprised of most of the women, were also to be stationed here in the command center, where the microphones and sound system would blast out the songs of praise as contained in the detailed daily listings. The prayer and intercessory team included Father Jake, a Catholic priest; Pastor Dave, a Protestant pastor; Rabbi Maskil, a Messianic Jewish rabbi; Irene, a retired nurse and wife of Moe; Diane, Rick's wife; Estelle, Bob's wife; Michelle, a teacher and wellness adviser and wife of Captain Gary; Anne, Pastor Dave's wife; Loren; Monique, Tom's wife; Forshia, Major Eric's wife; plus, Hailey, Joshua's wife.

The outside defense team at position 3 was under the command of George, the gas station / variety store owner, former gun dealer, and expert marksman; with Larry, a Marine sniper in Iraq; Richard, a retired schoolteacher; Sko, a retired school athletic director; and Gene, a former businessman, assigned to the area outside the command center and the path along the area leading to defensive position 2.

This area was also particularly important. It controlled the entire area from the first bend through the entire pass. It also connected positions 2 and 3. The defense area along this pass to the bend in the road was also heavily supplied with a multitude of items. Position 3 had a dozen heavy-duty storage trailers loaded with weapons, ammunitions, supplies, tents, provisions, and other items.

On the southern plateau of position 3 and along the small mountain passage leading to position 2, which had been carved out by Lieutenant Bernie's crew, was placed a catapult, a bulldozer, two larger front-end loaders, two small front-end loaders, barrel bombs, barrels and bottles filled with gasoline and ball bearings, barrels filled with rocks and sand, piles of riprap stones and eight-inch-minus stone, large rocks lined along the ledges between both positions, and another multitude of items that could serve as weapons or protective devices.

The soldiers and Lieutenant Bernie's crew had widened this small passageway to about twenty-five to forty-five feet wide, which allowed easy passage plus the ability to store a vast amount of materials and equipment.

These teams were to coordinate the defense efforts for both positions 2 and 3 between George's and Pierre's defensive positions. Initially, George's crew were to assist Pierre, and then Pierre's team was to assist George during the final battles.

It was anticipated that George's and Captain Gary's teams would also have to assist Rick's defensive position.

Fourth defensive position: western mountain command center (code word: WMC-04).

Above Moe's home and between the upper levels of position 6, one can see where the two mountain ranges met.

This position was Moe and Irene's mountain home, which was carved into the mountain and had great 270-degree view. Like George's home, Irene's home had a one-hundred-foot outdoor section to be used as a staging area to the south, and a seventy-foot staging area to the east. The interior of the home had nearly five thousand square feet of living space and two thousand square feet of storage, and it had its own electricity supply using solar power, with a backup diesel generator. This space would be used as a medical hospital and for food preparation by some of the ladies and a chef in addition to George's home.

Captain Gary, who had served in the Marines and Army and had also served in Iraq, was the defense coordinator for WMC-04 position 4. He was assisted by Moe, the business strategist. Gary's outside defense team also included Bob, a salesman; Jack, a former Navy SEAL and sniper in Vietnam; the five Bosnian men (Sajed, a toolmaker; Ruffard, a UPS driver; Humdia, a toolmaker and former Arman; Sade, a toolmaker; and Niaz, a heavy equipment mechanic).

We also placed a crane tow truck, and it had a large rope at its mask, which was used to lift the crosses at this position and used to pile some containers

Medical supplies and food provisions were under the direction of Jim, an EMT paramedic who also served in Vietnam as a medic; Rene, a former Army medic during the Vietnam War; Fran, Rene's wife; the wives of the five Bosnian men, being Zefina, Azama,

Merima, Fatima, and Ismeta; and Aboud, a Lebanese hummus shop owner.

Fifth defensive position: mountain road and pass (code word: MRP-05).

This involved the only road from the town south of us and going through the pass into the town. This position had three defenses: (A) the defense at the bend of the road approximately a thousand feet from the southerly mouth of the pass, (B) the defense at the southerly mouth of the pass, and (C) the defense at the northerly mouth of the pass, which was the "stand your ground" defense. There was also the fake defense layout between the last second defensive positions.

Looking out from Moe's southern ledge, we could see the second defensive position on the right and the raven and mountains on the left.

Mountain pass defense was under the command of Rick, former construction labor foreman and a former Marine during the Vietnam War. Assisting him in the defense of the road included Anthony, the owner of the closed concrete plant; Henry, the junkyard owner and former Army sergeant during the Vietnam War; Steve, an owner of the construction company; Ralph, an engineer; Peter, a distributor of construction materials, equipment, and parts; Carm, a construction superintendent; Nick, a construction superintendent; Jeremy, Larry, Sam, and Keith, four Marine expert marksmen who served in Vietnam with Rick.

The artillery and catapult defenses were organized by Vinko, a carpenter and medieval times buff; Jasmin, a Bosnian and the son of Niaz; Harry, the owner of the closed barrel manufacturing company; Lee, a hardware store owner and carpenter.

This was the key defensive position and had many supplies, especially at the final position at the entrance of the north portion of the pass. They had to defend the area from the first bend in the road, the entrance of the south pass, and along the entire pass through the entrance of the north pass.

Sixth defensive position: southwesterly mountain sniper position (code word: MSP-06).

This position was almost one thousand feet west of position 4 which, had a great view and would have direct view of the bend in the road, perfect for a sniper position, and would also have a view of the forest, river, swamp, and valley. They would oversee the forest defense and surveillance of the region to the west and assist in the defense of the road. This area had great easterly, southerly, and westerly views.

To the west of position 6 were lots of mountains, which made the area nothing but mountain ranges for nearly thirty miles, with rivers running between the mountains.

These mountain ranges formed a perfect defensive position, which the team did not have to defend. The farther west one went, the higher the mountain elevation became. It was virtually impossible to get over these mountains with equipment.

On a clear day, one could see the mountains' caps over thirty miles away.

This defense was under the command of Lou (a Vietnam vet who served as jungle fighter and explosive technician), with Normand (Vietnam jungle fighter and sharpshooter), Thomas (a woodsman), and Paul (a trapper) assisting him in defense and surveillance.

This defense was nearly impossible for the enemy to climb because the southerly face of the mountain went straight up for over twelve hundred feet from the base of the river and swamp to this staging area.

Two thousand square feet were carved out by the soldiers as a staging area on the northern side of the mountain just five feet below the peak of the mountain.

In addition, a pathway from this area to a level area 250 feet below was also prepared near the easterly side of that point. It was a great advantage for the sniper and for the grenade launcher, which weapons George had provided for the team. The grenade launchers were also provided for each of the other five team locations.

The catapults were stationed at all the defensive positions. The four additional slingshot types were also placed in the mountain positions of 2, 3, 4, and 5. The ten spring-action catapults were placed in positions 3, 4, 5B, and 5C. The team set up slides in order to roll the barrels off the mountaintop onto the advancing enemies. They were placed on position 1 (OP-1) in two locations (two on the southern ridge and the four others on the western ridge). Also on this position was placed a water buffalo filled with six thousand gallons of water, a hundred of the small barrels and propane tanks, a compressor, a power washer, two generators, tents, food provisions for a week, twenty thousand tons of riprap rocks, twelve-inch boulders, bowling balls, bows and arrows, pyrotechnic and rockets, blockbusters and cherry bombs, hand grenades and other explosives, pipes, and five flamethrowers supplied by the Amy. We placed a flamethrower at defensive positions 1 through 5.

Each of the six positions was equipped with one or two Bobcat front-end loaders and/or Bobcat forklift units to lift the barrels, rock, and other materials to either the catapults or the slides. We also placed a bulldozer at positions 2, 3, and 4 near the rocks placed near the walls. Along the perimeters of the mountain walls were boulders and riprap stones placed, which would easily be pushed to drop down the mountain onto the pass below, which also served as protective barriers. The two command centers also had a bulldozer and a larger front-end loader. These were lifted into position by the helicopter teams, as well as the catapults, storage containers, barrels, rocks, pipes, and whatever else were needed to fully supply the mountain positions according to the plan.

The teams set the light towers, message boards, and generators in positions 2, 3, 4, 5b, and 5c. The light towers were so bright they lit up the whole road up to the first bend. As one looked north, the lights were so blinding that no one could hardly see anything when they looked at our defensive positions.

Colonel John, Captain Gary, and Major Eric inspected all the defensive positions to ensure they complied with the Lord's plan. Every location had the proper number of defense items, ammunition, weapons, and escape routes. The teams tested all the various pieces of equipment and compared the plans given to us. They placed the final barriers in the roadway of the path from the south. At sunset, we gathered at George's for prayer and worship. Estelle opened with the song "Lord, I Need You, You Are My One Defense."

Rabbi Maskil read from chapter 4 of Philippians, which stated, "Renounce worry…do not be anxious…blessed is the man who believes in the Lord." He also read from Psalm 28, about the Lord being "my strength and my shield," and Psalms 92, "Have you not heard…my strength shall be renewed." Rabbi stated, "God wants us to come with our faith and trust in Him. We need to go to rest and get upon before sunup and assemble here. We need to pray from our hearts for increased faith. Through increased faith will we gain courage to do God's will without fear." Rabbi gave us the Aaronic blessing and dismissed us to our assigned positions. It was a perfect summer's eve.

THE FIRST OF THE
DAY OF DEFENSE

We woke up early, before sunrise, on the Fourth of July and went to George's gathering room just as the sun came over the mountain peaks. All the men except the members of the worship team were wearing military combat fatigues from the Army surplus store and some additional uniform had been supplied by Captain Mark's men. The officers of the command center wore their military dress uniforms, which included the metals and ribbons they had earned while serving. Moe wore the combat fatigue but had a sailor's hat on underneath his helmet in honor of his father who had been a career Navy man. The women and men who were part of the medic team wore medical-surgical garbs, and the food service team wore chef's attire and black uniforms they had gotten from the restaurants. Captain Roger wore his pilot's outfit and leather jacket. The worship team was wearing the church's worship robes of red, white, or blue. In hindsight, we really looked somewhat hysterical.

All were again gathered as we had done for seventy-three days. After prayer and worship, Rabbi Maskil read a verse from the Torah, from Isaiah 59:17–19: "For He put on righteousness as a breastplate and a helmet of salvation on His head; He put on the garments of vengeance for clothing and was clad with zeal as a cloak. According to their deeds, accordingly He will repay. Fury to His adversaries. Recompense to His enemies; the coastlands He will fully repay. So, shall they fear the Name of the Lord from the west, and His glory from the rising of the sun. When the enemy comes in like a flood, The Spirit of the Lord will lift a standard against him."

Pastor Dave rose up and said early that morning, the Lord gave him this passage while he was getting ready to come to church service; it was from Ephesians 6:10–20: "Finally, my brethren, be strong in the Lord and in the power of His might. Put on the whole armor of God that you may be able to stand against the wiles of the devil. For we do not wrestle against flesh and blood, but against principalities, against powers, against the rulers of darkness of this age, against spiritual hosts of wickedness in the heavenly places.

"Therefore, take up the whole armor of God that you may be able to withstand the evil day, and having done all, to stand. Stand therefore, having girded your waist with truth, having put on the breastplate of righteousness and having shod your feet with the preparation of the gospel of peace; Above all, taking the shield of faith with which, you will be able to quench all the fiery darts of the wicked one. And take the helmet of salvation and the sword of the Spirit, which is the Word of God, praying always with all prayer and supplication in the Spirit, being watchful to this end with all perseverance and supplication for all the saints—and for me, that utterance may be given to me, that I may open my mouth boldly to make known the mystery of the gospel, for which I am the ambassador in chains, that in it I may speak boldly, as I ought to speak."

Father Jake arose and said that he, too, received a scripture for us from Romans 8:26–32: "Likewise, the Spirit also helps in our weaknesses. For we do not know what we should pray for as we ought, but the Spirit Himself makes intercession for us with groanings which cannot be uttered. Now He who searches the hearts knows what the mind of the Spirit is, because He makes intercession for the saints according to the will of God. And we know that all things work together for good to those who love God, to those who are the called according to His purpose. For whom He foreknew, He also predestined to be conformed to the image of His Son, that He might be the firstborn among many brethren. Moreover, whom He predestined, these He also called; these He also justified; and whom He justified these He also glorified. What then shall we say to these things? If

God is for us, who can be against us? He who did not spare His own Son, but delivered Him up for us all, how shall He not with Him shall also freely give us all things."

Then Father Jake said to those gathered, "For it is written that we have fought the good fight of faith. Now is the time to be bold, because we have been called by the Lord for this predestined event, for such a time as this, to serve the Lord for His glory. He did not even spare His Son but glorified Him in three days, and through His glory, the Father was also glorified. We need to remember that these next few days will not be our battle, because the Lord planned out the entire events that will occur. We are called here to glorify Yahweh and His Son, our Lord Jesus, so that whatever takes place here, it is for His glory. We have been given a small part of what is to be played out, and we have been called to observe the awesome wonders of God. Some or all of us may be sacrificed, but the world will know that Yahweh and Jesus Christ are God and He still controls all the good things that go on in this world. As the Lord told Joshua, 'Do not fear and be courageous.' Remember what the Lord told us in 1 Corinthians 14:24–25: 'We know the end before the beginning. We have hope because we know the promise…declare that God is really among us.'"

Then Pastor Dave quoted Joshua 1:9: "Be strong and courageous, do not be afraid or discouraged, for the Lord your God will be with you wherever you go." And immediately we broke out in the Robin Mark song "When It's All Been Said and Done," and the congregation sang:

When it's all been said and done
There is just one thing that matters
Did I do my best to live for truth?
Did I live my life for you?
When it's all been said and done
All my treasures will mean nothing
Only what I've done
For love's reward
Will stand the test of time

Lord, your mercy is so great
That you look beyond our weakness
And find purest gold in miry clay
Turning sinners into saints

I will always sing your praise
Here on earth and ever after
For you've shown me heavens my true home
When it's all been said and done
You're my life when life is gone
When it's all been said and done
There is just one thing that matters,
Did I do my best to live for truth?
Did I live my life for you?

Then the pastor said, "We are the remnant. With Him I know we can stand in His promises. The battle is the Lord's, and we thank You for choosing us to stand with You. Lord, this one is all Yours. You have chosen the weak to confound the strong. You have selected us to glorify Your name. The name above all names. Lord, we ask for nothing, for our reward is giving glory unto you. As in Samuel chapter 17, 'There is not a cause greater than this!' When you feel weak or disheartened, focus upon the cross and call upon the heavenly host of angels of God for assistance."

Then the praise team led us with the song "How Great Is Our God." Rabbi stated, "Each of us has been given specific gifts, tasks, and assignments. Now is the time to go to our stations according to the plan given to us by our Lord. And remember, our call is to stand our ground. We need to execute our tasks with precision, and we need to coordinate our actions with command central. We need to remain in constant communications with command central, and we must act in timely unison and not jump the gun, because this will affect the outcome." Rabbi added, "Do not be afraid and be of great courage. May the Spirit of the Lord and His heavenly host protect us. Should any of us or all of us perish, it will be a glorious day, because we will be with the Lord Almighty as we did our duty to our very best to serve the Lord. For it is written in James 1:12, 'Blessed is the person who remains steadfast under trial, for when he stood the test, he will receive the crown of life, which God has promised to those who love Him.'"

Pastor Dave arose and said, "We will be tested over the next week. We need to focus upon the cross, which has been placed for all to see. Joshua has placed red, white, and blue lights so we can see them at night. Great strength comes from faith in God. Faith will overcome fear if you keep your focus upon the cross and not upon your immediate circumstances. You need to remember God's promises to us. God's hedge of protection is upon us, as written in Psalms 91:1–2, 11–12, 'He who dwells in the secret place of the Highest, shall abide under the shadow of the Almighty. I will say of the Lord, He is my refuge and my fortress; my God, in Him I will trust. For He shall give His angels charge over you, to keep you in all your ways. In their hands they shall bear you up.' Again, in 2 Corinthian 10:3–4, 'For if we walk in the flesh, we do not war according to the flesh. For the weapons of our warfare are not carnal but mighty in God for pulling down strongholds.' We are not fighting the fight. The battle is the Lord's. I agree with Rabbi Maskil: when you feel tired or when the situation looks bleak, look up to the cross and meditate upon the scriptures of the songs of praise and worship. Most of the praise-and-worship songs selected by our Lord were meant to lift you up during the trials so that you can keep your focus upon the cross and God's Word. Remember, you are a child of God, and in our Father's house, there is a place for each one of us." The worship team sang one last song, which started, "Amazing love, how can it be that you my King would die for me?"

We left the church, and Rick and Tom drove the buses along the road to the farthest easterly position, observation position 1. We all got out of the bus, and the prayer team led us back, praising and worshipping and consecrating the ground, the mountain, and the ravine. Pastor blessed each of the defensive positions, the men who were to defend them, the American and Israeli flags, and the bombs and debris placed alongside the road. We thanked God for allowing us to regain our health for this great opportunity and for the opportunity to service Him. We finished with a Communion service, and the pastors and rabbi blessed each one of us with anointing oil. All team members were given general absolution by Father Jake after praying the sinners' prayer. Rabbi Maskil and Pastor Dave stopped and said a special prayer over four of our Vietnam vets, separate from anyone else. We didn't know at that time what this meant or why they singled these four out from the rest of us; we just thought they need more prayer because they may experience flashbacks. We were sent back to our assigned position to recheck our supplies and go over our duties.

About an hour after the service, the teams were at each of their respective posts. Then the southern lookout saw six vehicles and two armored personnel carriers coming from the south, and they were brandishing the black-and-white ISISA flag.

The worship team started singing the assigned songs for the first day in a worship mode, and they cranked up the volume for the enemy to hear. The first songs were "Be Not Afraid," "Turn Your Eyes Upon Jesus," and "This Is the Day." They heard the songs. The second group of songs was all recognizable Hebrew and Israeli songs, which these Middle Eastern ISISA recognized, and this fired them up and really irritated them.

They sped up. First, the two armored personnel carriers aligned themselves alongside each other, which took up the whole road. Occasionally, they even hit the junk cars along the side of the road after they rounded the second bend. They became even more infuriated when they saw the Israeli flag next to the American flag and they jumped out of the pickup truck and ripped off the Israeli flag and burnt the first dozen or so, howling, "Allahu Akbar!" As they proceeded up the road, one of the soldiers from the last truck grabbed another Israeli flag to burn, to desecrate it, but this one was wired to a hand grenade attached to a barrel of gasoline with ball bearings, screws, and other small metal items. Three seconds later, the grenade exploded, which exploded the barrel, sending metal and fire everywhere, taking out that individual and the two trucks adjacent to him. The impact of the blast blew the two trucks off the road and over the cliff and down into the ravine seven hundred feet below. The blast was the opening event for the snipers and the sharpshooters to commence firing.

Those on the outpost of the second bend were to shoot at the rear guards on the truck manning the machine guns. Those manning the defense at the first bend in the road were to shoot at the drivers, and then the soldiers riding shotgun in trucks behind the personnel carrier first. Those manning the mountain position above the first bend were to focus upon the passengers in the vehicles. As bullets were flying, the armored carriers gunned it and barreled toward what they perceived to be the checkpoint and those firing upon them. They reached speeds of sixty miles an hour and careened into the checkpoint, and as they realized they were running over dummies and broke through the billboard, they were heading over the embankment and down into the ravine, where the two vehicles exploded when it hit the rocks near the base for the mountain. The rest of the team eliminated the twelve in the truck within the minute. Several members of Rick's team threw the bodies into the trucks and sent the trucks down into the ravine. They picked up any guns and ammunition from the trucks. They also picked up the four heavy-duty machine guns and related ammunition from the backs of the trucks and jeeps before they sent them over the cliff.

This first battle lasted less than three minutes, and the cleanup took less than twenty minutes. The team also threw all the remaining debris from the enemy over the embankment. They left the items with explosive devices intact in the road's bend. The machine guns were brought back to Rick's first defensive position and set up for the next battle. They placed two of the machine guns in the armored school bus, one in the back and one in the side. The snipers and sharpshooters performed with such great precision that the twelve were taken out with extreme accuracy. We did not know whether men in the armored carrier were able to communicate with their command center.

The notice was given that all was clear, and so the singing stopped after the song "Lord I Believe" by John Polce. We braced for a second round of attacks, but nothing occurred that day. It appeared that none of the fighters had been able to radio back to their command center. This was extremely important because we needed the element of surprise to be on our side.

At sundown, we could not all physically assemble, so we did so by using the computer, tablets, and radio communications. The ladies and pastors sang praises to the Lord and gave God the victory. We all sang praises to the Lord while at our stations and thanked the Lord for His protection as no one was injured or killed. They sang "Grace Comes Like a Wave" and finished with "Shine Your Light and Let the Whole World See the Glory of the Risen King." The men and women of the support team brought food and beverages to all the defense stations during the day and evening. We left the lights off except the lights on the cross and the streetlights from a mile before the south bend to the next village.

After the worship service, Captain Roger and his team sent up two of the drones to see where the enemy was located. They could tell that they were in the neighboring village to the south because we could see smoke continuously rising because they were burning many of the buildings. They flew almost to the maximum distance but saw no one and no movement in the area, which was almost five miles from the command center.

Josh and Captain Roger worked on attempting to modify some of the drones and planes to attempt to fly farther. They even attached certain of the Fourth of July rockets and flares on a couple of the planes to see if they could use them as a weapon.

Also, Tom, George, and few of the men used their downtime to make more bullets at George's secret workshop. Tom and George knew how to make bullets and guns, so they oversaw the operation and trained others from the service team.

The teams slept in shifts of four hours at their stations. Tents, sleeping bags, charcoal grills, coffee, and all other necessary items were previously brought to the stations the day before. The service team cooked and brought the food and beverages to each of the positions.

Rene and one of the team members also fabricated a stand like what one would use when lifting weights. This stand would help Rabbi Maskil keep his staff raised high during the battles. Many of the service team members and those with George worked with Tom and Rick to continue to make more bullets during their spare hours. We rechecked our supplies to be sure we had what we were assigned.

At dawn of the second day, Captain Roger's drone spotted approximately 240 or so armed men, a dozen various-size trucks, and one artillery piece trailing behind the larger truck, approximately three miles away, coming up the road. There were no armored vehicles, just trucks with ISISA soldiers in the rear of some of them and several pickup trucks with two men manning a machine gun in the rear of the truck. There appeared to be a man on the passenger side holding an automatic weapon. When the first vehicle of the caravan approached the second bend, the worship team started to sing songs of praise and songs of worship, just as listed in the plan, like, "Lord, I Want to Be a Christian" and "Just a Closer Walk with Thee" and "Lord of the Dance" and "Our God Reigns." They turned up the volume in the equipment to be sure the enemy would hear them. Then they sang a mixture of Jewish praise songs to Yahweh. They were singing like angels in true worship.

When the enemy heard the singing, they could not figure where the music was coming from, and they were getting really annoyed, especially when they were singing the Hebrew songs. They were moving around very cautiously. The men on foot jumped into the trucks until they were full, and the trucks formed a wall in front of the remaining men. The trucks drove three abreast, with about fifty men behind them, and there were four such rows of vehicles with the vehicle carrying the artillery in the rear position. The first row picked up speed and charged ahead; the second row delayed by waiting a minute or so until the fifty men were about a hundred feet ahead of them. The same happened for the third and the fourth rows of the vehicles and men. Each group was separated by 100 to 150 feet. This group of fighters looked more disciplined than the first group. The first of the four groups of the fighters was now approaching the first bend, and the others extended nearly 400 feet from the second bend in the road.

The worship team started to sing "Yahweh, I Know You Will Not Leave Me" and "I Believe in You, You Are the God of Miracles." The fighters were becoming irritated. The men started to break ranks and started pulling out the American and Israeli flags, and once again, three of the flags that were pulled were wired to hand grenades attached to barrels of gasoline, wiping away a half-dozen trucks and over eighty of the enemy troops. The sharpshooters and snipers started shooting at the enemy. They were shooting from four positions. The rear position was at the second bend, and their targets were that fourth group of fighters and artillery vehicle and the barrels closest to the troops near the second bend. Some of the fighters were attempting to climb the mountain to get to our defenders, but they started to roll barrels with rocks and the smaller barrels with gasoline and metal down the hill. The barrels with the gasoline were in the middle of several fighters when the sniper shot the barrel and a great explosion occurred, which blew away anyone within a hundred feet of the barrel. The snipers commenced shooting the barrels and the propane tanks near the fighters, and the explosions were systematically wiping out dozens of fighters at a time.

The groups in the mountain at the first bend commenced doing the same, and Rick, Tom, and the rest of their team moved the bus stationed near the first bend, which had steel plates fashioned on left side. Four of the men moved the bus back across the road and opened fire with the machine guns, grenade rocket launchers, and began shooting the fighters with their own guns and ammunitions. The team on the hill from position 2 also had men from the command centers lobbing grenades, firing bazookas, and using their M16s from the hill behind the rocks. Another group from position 3 also started to drop barrels and propane tanks upon the fighters as the snipers, sharpshooters, and expert shooters shot at the barrels and tanks right when they were a dozen feet away from the fighters or the trucks. The explosions caused chaos among the fighters. The fighters were trapped between the first bend and the second bend in the road, and our guys were picking them off as in a turkey shoot. They were confused and dropping like flies and in total disarray. Our shooters at the first bend on the bus were picking off the drivers and guards of the first-row vehicles, while the shooters on the mountain near the first bend were picking off the fighters and the drivers of the second and third group of vehicles.

The shooters at the second bend were taking out the last group systematically, and Captain Roger and his team, with the use of his drones and planes, were keeping tabs on the enemy plus were exploding the barrels and tanks between the third and fourth enemy groups, cutting them down with tons of flying metal and debris. They were blowing up the barrels and tanks on the mountain cliff, and every fourth detonation came from the mountainside, blowing the trucks and the men over the cliffs. Their fighters were running around in circles.

Position 6 was using the catapult to lob five- and fifteen-gallon barrels with metal ball bearings to the fighter positions, and their sharpshooters would shoot the barrel about ten feet above the fighters. The fight lasted an hour and twenty minutes. Most of the trucks were blown off the road into the ravine below because of the mountainside blasts. Roger's drones circled above and could not see anyone moving. No one had escaped, and body parts were all over the road. Eight destroyed trucks were sideways in the road. The worship team just finished singing "How Great Thou Art." We stopped shooting when there was nothing left to shoot at. Rick and Tom advanced with their men to clear up the debris and brought whatever ammunition, guns, and other usable arms to George. He brought in the bulldozer and tow truck to clear the road and push the debris over the cliff, including the dead bodies.

There were two gravely wounded fighters who attempted to grab their guns, but they were shot in that attempt by one of Rick's men.

In two days, we killed nearly three hundred fighters and destroyed over thirty trucks, two armored personnel carriers, and one piece of artillery. We did not lose anyone of our members, and no one was injured. We praised God for all His planning and all His deeds. No one rejoiced in the carnage or the deaths of these misled fighters. At dusk, we worshipped and praised God for all He did and prepared for the next day by taking stock of our needs.

THE THIRD DAY

A t sunrise on the third day, our service team brought breakfast and supplies. We prayed and worshipped using the loud-speakers, which everyone could hear, and each team joined our ladies and pastors in songs of praise at their respective station.

At around eight in the morning, the most westerly side, position 6 lookout, while scouting the area with binoculars, spotted dozens of armed men going into the woods south of the marshes and pond near the foot of the mountain. He radioed command center, where Captain Roger, Joshua, and their team sent up a drone and two planes to see what was up. He confirmed that there were between thirty and forty armed men entering the woods from the cavern. They came in several small boats and disembarked in the field near the forest. Captain Roger directed one of his planes to follow the river, and they saw another thirty boats carrying six men in each boat, going farther downriver, heading north. Captain Roger connected with Captain Mark eighty miles away to let them know that ISISA fighters were going upstream, and he sent their current location. Captain Mark indicated that they had three gunboats on the river and they would intercept the thirty boats. Captain Roger told Captain Mark that in two days of fighting, we had destroyed nearly three hundred fighters and numerous assets of the enemy. He indicated that they were now trying to circumvent the pass and to find an alternate way to attack our positions.

We were not worried about those on the river, because the mountain range went on for over thirty miles and the mountains' heights continued to increase each mile until they were over 3,500 feet above the cavern. The next ten miles had a drop-off of the mountain ledges, which were significant and almost vertical, thus impossible to climb, unless one was an experienced professional mountain climber with the proper mountain climbing equipment. The fighters were sent out as scouts to locate an alternate route and a point of weakness in our defenses. They did not know the terrain. The government had GPS, Google Map, and similar services turned off to everyone except the military.

Lou and his team had an idea to distract those fighters; they suggested that someone go to the clinic or hospital and pick up all the blood packets and sprinkle them in the woods to attract the wild animals. So we sent the EMT and nurse to get the blood. Captain Roger and one of the engineers designed a device to attach the blood to the plane, and it would drain the bag of blood on demand. They sent up the first plane and sprinkled the central part of the woods with blood to attract the animals.

We did not know if this would work, but we were relying more upon God's plan as to what was already set up in the woods. After executing this plan, we started to think if we did something wrong because this was not in God's plan and we were now implementing our own thoughts into the defense. We did do one other major blunder: we forgot to repent.

As the fighters entered the woods or forest, they started to encounter the various traps set up by the Vietnam vets based upon that unique form of defense. As the fighters proceeded into the woods, the security cameras hidden within the stuffed owls were able to pick up their motions and the directions in which the fighters were going. The soldiers were proceeding in rows of twelve. They were headed toward the marsh area. When the woods became much thicker, the fighters began walking into the traps. As they pushed through the thickets, seven of the twelve got hit by the bungee sticks coming across, hitting them in the back. They were dead instantly. The fighters did not know what to do, yet they proceeded forward farther into the woods, and others fell into small pits, piercing their feet or their hands, resulting in excruciating pain. Only half of the fighters made it through the woods and dragged the wounded to the marshes' edge. Two of the fighters started to wade through the marshes, and they were being bitten by the fish and started to bleed, which attracted the other carnivorous fish and the alligators in the marsh. Through the activity in the marsh, more than a dozen poisonous snakes left their nest and attacked the fighters. Three of the fighters were bitten and started swelling up and passed out. The fighters who had stepped upon the bungee sticks were bleeding badly. A band of wolves caught the scent and was at the edge of the woods, each of them looking at their next meal. When the fighters saw the animals and heard a bear, they started to panic. They abandoned those being eaten up by the fish, those who had walked upon the bungee sticks, and the three bitten by the snakes and started to run back into the woods. As they did so, they ran into other traps and stepped upon explosive devices, which blew them up. Only two of the fighters made it back to the river. They got into the boat and went south back to their camp.

There were no clouds in the sky this day, and Joshua was flying one of the drones on the west slope when he spotted a few dozen fighters climbing the mountain about two thousand feet west of position 6. This was just out of reach of the position 6 snipers. Captain Roger was flying his model plane on the east side about twenty-five hundred feet east of position 1. Captain Roger spotted nearly fifty fighter three-quarters of the way up the mountain slope. Both locations were thought of as not being climbable. They communicated this to Colonel John and Major Eric. They did not know what they should do. They did not have enough time to send any defenders to the area. This was not in the plan. Rabbi said, "We need to trust in God."

Pastor Dave heard them talking and went back to the praise-and-worship room and told the team to pray to our Lord for guidance and assistance. Some of the team members had been just singing the song "I Believe in You, the God of Miracles" when the pastor came into the room. The other half of the team began praying in tongues, and the sound was angelic. The praying went over the sound system, and Pastor Dave announced that all church members pray in tongues. The worship team started to sing "The Spirit Is A-moving" and "Peace Is Flowing Like a River" and, finally, "Let It Rain." This situation was not in the playbook of the Lord, but it did say, when all else fails, trust in the Lord of hosts.

The worship team was quickly assembled. They started their third-day worship songs according to plan. The worship team just started to sing "Go Tell It on the Mountain" when a cloud came from nowhere. Pastor Dave looked out of the northern window from George's home and saw a large black cloud coming over the horizon from the northwest. It was moving fast toward our defensive positions. The worship team was now singing "Rocka My Soul." Before the cloud reached defensive position 6, the cloud started to split in half. The rear portion of the cloud hovered on the north side of the mountain nearly a quarter mile west of our western defensive position.

Just as the prayer team started to sing "It's Me, Oh Lord, Standing in the Need of Prayer," the other half of the cloud sped up and passed the command center and headed directly past the position 1 outpost, toward the area where the fighters were climbing. As the clouds reached where the fighters were, just then, both clouds circled and moved directly over the fighters climbing the mountain at both locations. The worship team just started to sing "Joy Is Like the Rain," and suddenly, a humungous gust of wind, lighting, and a downpour of both water and hail came forth from the clouds. The worship team was now singing "The Battle Hymn of the Republic" when the rain made the rocks very slippery and the hail the size of baseballs began hitting the fighters and knocking them off the mountain. The gust of wind blew many of the fighters off the mountain. After twenty minutes of this, Captain Roger and Joshua sent out their drones and planes to the area and could not locate one fighter. God fought that battle for us. The songs of praise, like, "Ho, Ho, Ho, Hosanna" and "Praise Ye the Lord," rang all over the mountains, and we thanked God for all He had done.

The service team brought food and beverages to each position, starting with the east lookout and the western lookout positions first, and then positions 2, 5, 3, and 4. This team worked awfully hard to meet our physical needs. They also brought bread and wine to be partaken at Communion at the appointed hour. At around one thirty in the afternoon, Pastor Jake, via the intercom system, announced a worship service and the breaking of the bread would take place. The worship team sang "Take Our Bread," followed by "Let Us Break Bread Together." After Father Jake's benediction, we sang "Jesus Is My Lord" and "We Thank You, Father." The last song we prayed was "He Has Made Me Glad."

Three minutes later, around two in the afternoon, the eastern outlook position 1 spotted a tank coming from the south. They radioed command center, and Captain Roger and his team sent up a drone and two planes and they were sent into different directions so that, if detected, they would not easily figure out where the drone or planes came from. They spotted two tanks, two armored carriers, and twenty pickup and passenger trucks with soldiers in the back of the trucks. Behind these vehicles were many more soldiers. Captain Roger's and his team's best estimate was that the fighters were in excess of four hundred, not counting the soldiers in the trucks and the armored personnel carrier. They were about thirty minutes away from the second bend in the road and moving at about four miles per hour.

The other teams were notified, and we had to review our options and timing according to the design and remaining explosives between the first and second defensive positions. Colonel John and Captain Gary reread the defense plans for the third day and now realized what God had told them earlier, which was not professionally written down into the plan. Someone neglected to write down the sequence of the defense plans. They had everything written down but neglected to identify the order of how to execute the plan. They called in the rabbi, pastors, and worship team and asked them to pray to identify the order of what we were to do.

They started to pray in tongues, and within five minutes, Irene and Estelle started to speak alternately. "The Lord said, 'Do not fear, and be of great courage. You are wise to consult with Me when you make an error. This is what you are to do, and now, write this down and communicate this with all positions. Do nothing until the tanks reach the first bend. You planted explosives in the drains near the first bend, so they will be the first detonated by Lieutenant Bernie and his team just as the first tank reaches the front of the bend. Explode the three detonation positions from the first bend, heading toward the second bend. The signal is to be when the worship team starts to sing "Give Me Oil in My Lamp." When that occurs, that will be the sign for all individuals from positions 1 and 2 to commence dropping the barrels and for the snipers to shoot the barrels and the tanks along the mountainside of the road. Position 6 shall catapult their medium- and smaller-size barrels with the metal in increments of one minute. Use maximum range when firing the catapults. When fighters commence climbing the mountain, roll the round rocks and riprap off the mountain and send ten barrels of oil down the hill from different locations near defensive position 1 and defensive position 2 and remove the lids before sending them down the hill. Team from defensive position 3 shall advance and assist defensive position 2.

"'Defensive position 5 shall advance to the bend, first using the bulldozer and the front-end loader to push the first tank over the cliff. Men shall also advance with the bulldozer and loader to defend the operators. Bring the bus with four men from the team to man the machine guns and place the bus between the bus and the dozer as soon as the first tank has been pushed over the cliff. Have someone throw a grenade into the gun barrel of the second tank and two grenades immediately behind the tank. The second defensive position needs to throw two barrels of gasoline and metal behind the second tank, and just before they hit the ground, the sniper and expert shooters shall shoot the barrels to explode them.'"

The Lord continued, "After defensive position explodes two barrels behind the second tank, the dozer and the loader operator shall advance toward the second tank and, using a strong chain and hook, link the tank and pull the tank forward to a position behind the bus and then push the tank over the cliff. You will need one machine gun operator to assist you during this operation.

"The first defensive position shall lob ten barrels of gasoline and metal, which you called barrel bombs, into the middle of the fighters, while others need to throw twelve grenades thirty seconds apart at the foot of the hill at the first bend for a distance of two hundred feet. Roll down twelve barrels containing riprap rocks, which you called rock barrels, down the face of the hill when fighters start climbing the hill. Then, roll down twelve barrels of oil from that location, heading in different directions, with the lid of the barrels removed, toward any fighters remaining on the mountain face. The sharpshooters and snipers shall shoot at barrel bombs and propane tanks alongside the mountain, as marked, to blow away fighters over the cliff along with any trucks. The fighting will last 150 minutes. When all is silent, clear off the road with the bulldozer and the front-end loader. Fear not and have great courage, for I am with you."

Colonel John immediately distributed the orders to the commanders of each position as to the sequence of what needed to be done. The worship team started singing "He's Got the Whole World in His Hands." The tanks had just passed the second bend, heading toward the first bend in the road. The worship team commenced their singing songs of praise, which blasted through the dozens of loudspeakers hidden in the mountain. The next song they sang was "Yahweh," followed by "Oh How I Love Jesus." The fighters looked around but saw no one. The teams prepared to execute their part of the plan while they waited for the tanks to reach the first bend in the road and the detonation of the explosives by Lieutenant Bernie's team. The security cameras located at defensive position 3 were able to see when the tanks came into view at the bend in the road.

Just as the worship team started to sing "Give Me Oil in My Lamp," they viewed the base of the tank reaching the bend. Lieutenant Bernie's team detonated the explosives in the drain basins just under the first tank, and then followed by the second drain basins, and the last in the sewer basin, just under the second tank. These were massive explosions, with the first tank being blown to the edge of the cliff and the second tank significantly damaged, and the trucks were blown off, but the gun was still workable. The troops behind the tank were sent flying everywhere, and many over the cliff. Position 2 commenced dropping the barrels as the bus and the bulldozer with the loader came out in unison and pushed the first tank over the cliff. Rick's team was in the bus and started firing the machine guns taken from a previous fight as the fighters started to advance toward the bus. There were at least fifty fighters now behind the tank, which was on fire when position 2 dropped their barrels and barrel bombs onto their positions, with the snipers blowing them up just as the barrels reached the fighters. And after both barrels exploded, the two explosions eliminated not only the fifty fighters but a portion of the others a hundred feet away as well. Immediately thereafter, Rick and Tom ran toward the tank and threw a hand grenade down the barrel of the tank and ran behind the bus just as the grenade exploded, which caused another explosion in the tank, which rocked the tank. The man ran to the tank and attached the metal chain with a hook on it to the tow truck and the bulldozer, which pulled the tank forward. The bus protected the front-end loader while they pushed the tank over the cliff. Rick said he could hear the worship team start blasting out "Do Lord, Do Remember Me" and prayed He would remember him and his team.

Positions 1 and 6 commenced lobbing additional barrels as directed, which landed in the midpoint of the fighters, causing much damage and great confusion among the fighters. Position 2 was also lobbing barrels, and the snipers there were shooting propane tanks on the cliffside of the road, while snipers from position 1 were shooting propane tank and barrels with the gasoline and metal on the mountainside of the road. Several fighters attempted to scale the mountain near positions 1 and 2. The teams put the barrels with stones onto the slides and lifted the slides, and the barrels of rocks went down the mountain, spilling the riprap as it went down the mountain, hitting many of the fighters. They each sent twelve barrels of rocks this way and then commenced sending the barrels of oil down the mountain. The oil spilled onto the rocks, and when the fighters attempted to scale the mountain, they slid down the mountain and struck their heads against the rocks near the base of the mountain, and many died.

With all this activity going on simultaneously, and with all the metal ball bearings, screws, and other metal pieces flying around, hitting the fighters, they were in total confusion, and as they attempted to run back toward their camp, they were cut down by the sharpshooters and marksmen, while the snipers focused upon hitting the propane tanks or barrel bombs near the fighters. The fighting was intense and lasted for nearly ten minutes shy of two hours before we noticed that all was silent. We could hear the praise team singing "Great Things Happen When God Mixes with Us."

Although several fighters attempted to run, no one escaped. Over 450 fighters, twenty trucks, two armored carriers, and two tanks were destroyed. The carnage was so bad that certain members of the team became sick at the sight. The smell of burnt flesh with gasoline charring everything now became difficult for some of the team members. The worship team was just finalizing "Put Your Hand in the Hand" when the fighting ceased, and all were dead.

Rick's team came out with automatic weapons, while the bulldozer and front-end loader pushed all the debris and bodies over the cliff into the ravine, which was seven hundred feet below. This time it took nearly three hours to clean up the debris. We had three large holes in the road where the water drain and sewer drain had been. Rick's team repaired the road and filled it in with rock, riprap, and sand. They took the sand from the temporary defense just around the first bend. Another demolition team member also placed the barrel bombs and plastic explosive and buried them under the sand and wired the explosives to Lieutenant Bernie and Captain Roger's defensive position 3 with the remaining wire left.

Half of the teams, except for the first lookout position, and two members of position 6 gathered at command center at sundown for praise and worship. As we started our praise songs, Father Jake had the communications team switch up the loudspeakers so that the lookouts could hear and participate in the worship. We thanked Yahweh for all He had done for us and for protecting us with His heavenly host. We thanked Jesus, His only Son, for dying on the cross and for His sacrifice for all of us sinners. We prayed that Yahweh would have mercy on the fighters we had to kill. We repented to have killed anyone and so many, but we had no choice, nor did we delight in it.

About an hour later, while we were finishing up our Communion service, a call from position 1 indicated that they heard something out there. Rabbi Maskil gave us the Aaronic blessing, and we went off to our posts. Position 1 had such a difficult time handling all they had to do, so two members of Lou's team went to help position 1. Captain Roger and his team sent one drone and two planes with cameras up into the sky but could not see anything because it was very dark, almost pitch-black, because the moon was just a small crescent. The people at the first defensive position asked if they should send up any flares or pyrotechnics to light up the sky, and Captain Roger confirmed to do so without conferring with Colonel John or with the plan. They sent up the flares, which lit up the area beyond the third bend in the road from the village in which the fighters were coming from. Josh had also wired the mountain with floodlights during the three days of preparation and notified command center.

While the service team and medical team were feeding our group, Colonel John ordered all the floodlights to be turned on from position 1 through position 4. The drones and planes spotted a massive movement of what had to be over a thousand fighters with fifty various-size trucks and armored carriers in front and alongside them. They did not see any tank. The troops were almost up to the third bend in the road. Position 1 kept sending up the flares as well as Captain Roger from the planes, and the configuration of the enemy was six armored carrier in the front, six trucks with machine gunners in place, six fighters abreast, with a truck or an armored vehicle on each side for protection.

There were over one hundred rows of fighters, which extended over a mile. All in all, there must have been twelve hundred fighters coming toward us in the pitch-black dark, wearing black uniforms. Good thing for the lighting and the fireworks. Some of us started to fear, and sensing this, Rabbi Maskil, Father Jake, and Pastor Dave, and Irene and a few other ladies, started to sing songs of praise, which contained words like, "Fear not, Yahweh is with you," and our people started to regain composure and to buckle down to do what we were called to do. They started to sing "I Will Call Upon Your Name and You Will Deliver Me." Father Jake read the scripture from Job, citing "God's hedge of protection over us."

Colonel John's team went over the game plan for this next wave, and with confidence and trust in our Lord, we took our positions except for two of the men from position 6, who took it upon themselves to assist position 1 in the battle. In hindsight, they were not following God's playbook, and that was not a good thing. Position 1 and these two were not trusting in the Lord and were supplanting their own opinions and desires over the wisdom of the Lord. Colonel John was not notified that the two had gone to the first defensive position.

Rick's team went ahead and placed the bus, the bulldozer, and the 980G front-end loader at the second bend in the road, blocking the road. With the tow truck, they also moved concrete blocks and debris from the junkyard in front of the bus, dozer, and loader for twenty feet to make it harder for their armored carriers to ram the defense line. His team also placed several barrel bombs sprayed with fluorescent green of various sizes seventy to a hundred feet behind this debris for the snipers to hit.

The company of fighters reached the second bend in the road and heard the worship team blaring out the praise songs using the names of Yahweh and Jesus, and they became incensed. They sang "Jesus Loves Me" and "Jesus, Won't You Come by Here?" The company started to pick up the pace, and they were heading toward the first bend. The lead vehicles saw the blockade and quickened the pace even more. The armored vehicles started to fire upon the bus and other equipment, and when they reached two hundred feet from the bend, command center fired several pyrotechnic flares and turned on all the floodlights between positions 1 and 2, which lit up the sky and the whole area. The demolition team simultaneously blew up four of the larger bombs hidden in the sewer and water drains, destroying two-thirds of the armored vehicles in the front row and several trucks in the next two rows all at once.

When the praise team started singing "Where You There When They Crucified My Lord," then positions 1, 2, 3, and 6 commenced lobbing the stone barrels and barrel bombs in alternate sequence while the snipers, sharpshooters, and marksmen fired upon the barrel bombs and tanks along the mountain edge and a few along the cliff.

Rick's team opened fire with the machine guns, grenade launcher, and hand grenades. Team 4 continued to light up the sky with flares for the sharpshooters and snipers and dropped mortars on the midsection of the fighters. The fighters started to storm mountain positions 1 and 2, but with the assistance from the teams for positions 3, 5, and 6, they were able to roll the barrels of oil and the barrels of rocks down the mountain onto the fighters' positions. They also rolled a few barrels with just gasoline down the mountain, and then lit the fuel on fire, devastating dozens of fighters by setting them ablaze. There was wave after wave of fighters. Between the floodlights, pyrotechnics, flares, and flames from the barrel bombs, the dark night became very bright, and we could see all their movements.

The fighters were dropping like flies, but they just kept on coming. Rick's team pulled the dozer and loader back, and then the bus behind the bend. They parked them near the mountainside of the road in front of the next defensive position, 5a. Lou and the team from position 6 kept firing the bazooka and mortar rounds toward the remaining debris and the attacking fighters. They lowered their range and commenced dropping the barrel bombs onto the bend area and two hundred feet beyond the bend, just past the burning armored vehicles. Despite this barrage of fire, several fighters turned the bend, only to be met with a barrage of bullets from position 5a, and they were cut down as soon as they rounded the bend.

Moe and his team from position 4 assisted Rick's team using barrel bombs and barrels with oil via the catapults, grenades using the grenade launchers, which were taken from the previous battle, and firing rockets and flares to illuminate the skies for the other teams. The worship team commenced singing "Sing Hallelujah to the Lord," followed by "Swing Low," which the teams drew strength from.

The demolition team, with the help of Josh and Captain Roger, kept tabs on the fighters near position 1 to prevent them from retreating and to stop them from climbing the mountain. When several groups in the rear of the battalion attempted to retreat with a couple of armored vehicles and several trucks, they blew the plastic explosives in the drains and the barrels of metal on top of them, which were place in the sewer and water drains in the road. This took out not only the vehicles but also a couple hundred fighters behind them.

The fighters tried to climb the mountain near positions 1 and 2, but by now it was so slippery because of the oil and they kept falling off the mountain and getting injured or injuring others beneath them. The team on positions 1 and 2 continued to roll barrels of oil down the mountain, then barrels of gasoline and rocks, and finally a barrel bomb, alternating the bomb for every third barrel fired of the others. The worship team was singing "Jesus, Won't You Come by Here?"

The battle raged for over three hours, and we started to tire from killing so many people. Moe said he could hear the praise song, which gave their team the strength to continue as the worship team sang, "Lord, I come, I confess. Bowing here, I find my rest. Without You I fall apart. Lord, I need You, my one defense, my righteousness."

The shooting slowed to a trickle after the fourth hour. It was still very dark, but the floodlights really helped, and we stopped firing the flares after hour 3. The fighting was reduced to the snipers, marksmen, and sharpshooters and Captain Roger's drone and plane team, who attempted to identify anyone trying to escape or attempting to attack one of the positions. Captain Roger would often dive bomb fighters to try to get them to move or stand up, so the snipers would take them out. He lost two planes in doing so. The praise team was singing "Alle, Alle" during these last skirmishes.

Rick and five members of his team got back into the armored bus with the machine guns and ammunition and drove the bus back into position at the bend. The remainder of the team stayed at defensive position 5a for support or until Rick motioned to advance.

The sporadic shooting lasted until dawn, which enabled us to pick them off one at a time. The praise team's last song was "Morning Has Broken," just as the sun broke over the east mountain. A few fighters attempted to surrender, but the snipers from position 1 shot them anyway. It was now six in the morning of the fourth day, and the sun was a beautiful red.

Rick's bulldozer operator and 980G loader operator commenced cleaning up the debris and bodies behind the bus first and pushed everything over the cliff. After the bend was clear, the bus moved closer to the mountain, allowing the dozer and loader to begin clearing the front of the bus and pushing the debris and bodies into the ravine. Several members with automatic weapons from each of the team started to move down the road before the equipment. Other members joined them to pick up usable weapons and ammunitions for the next battle. We picked up a few additional high-powered machine guns for Rick's defensive positions, grenades, grenade launchers, ammunition, and other usable items.

During this process, one of the team members heard noises coming from one of the armored vehicles. He motioned to the front-end loader to push the vehicle over the cliff, and they did. The debris was so great and the bodies so numerous it was becoming tiring. It took four hours to clear off all the debris and bodies. All the vehicles were destroyed or blown over the embankment down into the ravine.

We looked at the chard, oil-soaked mountainside, but we decided not to do anything with it. Some of Rick's and Moe's team started to patch the large holes in the road caused by the sewer and drains being blown up with the plastic explosives and barrel bombs. They filed them in with rocks, sand, and gravel from the mountain. The demolition teams placed other explosives and barrels in the holes, and other team members brought out additional barrel bombs and propane tanks and strategically placed the barrels among the remaining debris left in position and positioned them to cause maximum damage.

We were exhausted and sick to see the carnage we had to endure. Only a few soldiers who served in the recent wars were not affected. A couple of the Vietnam War vets seemed to get invigorated by the action. We prayed for those two. We hoped that they were not enjoying the killing but only doing what they had to do. Rick moved the bus, the loader, and the dozer back into position just around the bend. We went back to the command center to pray, praise, and thank the Lord for all He had done.

So far, none of the seventy were either killed or wounded. We had killed nearly two thousand of the enemy and destroyed countless armored vehicles, tanks, and trucks.

Several of us gathered at George's to build more bullets, while the bounty of what was picked up was distributed based upon need, but much went to Rick's group.

We thanked the worship team for their praising and worshipping during the entire battle and the early morning. Their singing encouraged us at the right time. The service team and the medical team assisted in preparing breakfast for all of us and brought the lookout teams theirs at their positions. The kept us supplied with all our needs.

W e started to sleep in two shifts again, each sleeping four hours. Captain Roger and his team took shifts flying the drone and planes to watch for the next wave of attackers. We refurbished our supplies and then rested until late afternoon.

Some members were eagerly awaiting the arrival of our military, for which Captain Mark promised to return by late morning after the fourth day. It was now eleven in the morning, and as the command center looked toward the north, a call came in from the east watchmen notifying us that over four more divisions of armed men exceeding two thousand fighters, three tanks, six armed carriers, and dozens of trucks were on the road, heading toward us, approximately four miles away. The drone spotted another ten to twelve divisions camping just outside at the lake region five miles away. One of Joshua's planes was shot down by one of their fighters.

The Army did not come today, but some members prayed that they would come before nightfall or during the fight. Apparently, they did not remember one of the words given by Irene, which stated they would not come in time. Yet some interpreted that statement as being that they would not be here on day 3 and assumed it would be on day 4. We woke up the remaining members who were still asleep, and we went to our posts. Again, two of Lou's team members did not go to their post but instead went to position 1 with Aaron's group. This time, Colonel John asked them to report to their proper post, and they responded that they wanted to be where the action was and not in a supporting role. These were the same two who seemed to enjoy what they were doing. They also were the same individuals who shot those fighters as they were surrendering. They said they would return to position 6, but they did not.

At milepost 3, the three tanks pulled into the point positioned in a triangle formation, followed by two hundred fifty armed fighters, then three armored vehicles, followed by a dozen pickup trucks with two machine gun operators in the back, five hundred armed fighters, followed by a dozen trucks, followed by another five hundred fighters, then another three armored vehicles with another dozen pickup trucks, followed by six hundred armed soldiers, and lastly, another dozen pickup trucks and supply trucks and another thirty soldiers in jeeps, with nearly a hundred armed soldiers surrounding the jeeps. Our first thought was, this last group might be some of the higher-ranking officers, protected by hundreds of soldiers. They might have come to see why the other soldiers had not returned. No one ever escaped the previous battles. Maybe they thought the fighters might have deserted or just kept moving north.

Colonel John called the command team and communicated the plan to the rest of the positions. This was the largest group so far, and we did not know whether there was enough room to fit all the vehicles, tanks, and troops within the space between the second bend and the first bend.

Colonel John and Major Eric called Rick to bring the bus, dozer, and loader back to position 5a, according to the designed plan, which was halfway between the bend in the road and the southerly entrance of the mountain pass. He sent four of his men to the area between positions 2 and 3. Captain Gary commanded the team to the south wall of position 4, and Moe commanded the east wall of position 4, where the catapults, mortar, and grenade launchers were positioned.

Rick had given Pierre all the rocket-propelled grenades that his men had mustered from the fighters. Rick divided the automatic guns and ammunition gathered among the teams with the most need.

The praise-and-worship teams commenced their singing of "Amazing Grace," and then they started to sing in tongues, which had a marked effect upon the front portion of the advancing fighters. It was hilarious to see the confusion, their looking around as if someone had whispered in their ears. They stopped their vehicles, and their officers wanted them to continue moving forward and kept hollering at them to keep moving. The officer even shot one of them when he did not do so. Even the tank drivers stopped for several minutes for no apparent reason. One of the officers went over to the lead tank and opened the hatch and ordered them to move, and they started to roll again. The tanks reached the second bend and saw the chard mountainside and the road condition. As tanks advanced toward the first bend, Vinko and those manning the catapults loaded up, awaiting the orders. So did the other catapult operators. On the mountains, they prepared the slides and jacks to roll the barrels of oil and barrels of gasoline down the hill. Captain Gary, in charge of position 4, and George's crew, in position 3, including those along the ridge going to defensive position 2, prepared their defenses while awaiting the signal. Captain Roger and Josh kept tabs of the advancing troops with their drones and planes, getting a bird's-eye view of the enemy's positions and advancements.

The worship team started to loudly sing the song "In the Name of Jesus," followed by the "Desert Song." The loudspeakers and the mountains magnified the sound in such a way that the troops could not determine where the sounds were coming from because the songs were bouncing off the mountains. Every time the worship team sang the name Jesus, the soldiers became irritated and aggressive.

As the tanks were approaching the first bend, Rick, Tom, and two of his men hiding behind the bus were awaiting the orders to proceed to lob grenades in the tank's turrets. The 980G loader bucket was awaiting all three tanks to begin to make their turn heading toward position 5a. Colonel John was to have one rocket fired into the air to have the catapults release their barrel bombs from position 3, just behind the tanks, and position 2 was to drop the barrel bombs from the slides onto the positions one hundred feet from the bend to the point of the bend. Positions 1 and 6 were to maximize the distance with their catapult barrel bombs, while positions 4 and 5 were to focus on the tanks, armored carriers, and trucks, and the troops behind the tanks once they cleared the first bend in the road.

Colonel John saw the first tank come through, and the front of the second and third tanks was just in view. The first tank started to pivot in the road and was just about in direct line with our first defense five hundred feet away.

The tank closest to the mountain was just starting its pivot when the signal was given by Colonel John and the rocket flare was sent up for all to see. The teams commenced firing, and the barrel bombs were flying in the air. Vinko's first bomb hit just behind the tank and took out many soldiers and an armored vehicle. Team 6 discharged their barrel bombs, hitting just past the bend, taking out other soldiers and several pickup trucks and another armored vehicle. At that point, Rick, Tom, with their two team members, rushed the tanks and threw grenades down the turrets of the tanks. As the first tank opened to fire, the grenades exploded the shell inside the turret, which exploded and destroyed the turrets and the interior of the tanks. All three tanks were destroyed, and they now were blocking the other vehicles from coming around the bend.

Rick and the other team members went back to the bus and the bulldozer and inched the bus as close as it could to the rear tank. The dozer pushed the first tank over the cliff. Then they attempted to push the other tank on the right side of the road closer to the other tank to block the road at the bend, to prohibit the fighters from shooting at defensive position 5a. The defense team in the bus was to pin down the fighter near the bend in the road. They initially fired rocket-propelled grenades at the trucks behind the tanks, which sent the soldiers flying.

The position 2 team kept lobbing barrels with rocks and the barrel bombs in the area of the bend to keep the fighters away while they repositioned and moved the tanks. After positioning the tank, they lifted the tank onto its side with the 980G loader, with a five-yard bucket and with the help of the dozer operator. They also tipped the tank over onto its left side and pushed it back beyond the bend. The bus backed up against the tanks, completely blocking the road and enabling it to fire upon the fighters from the bus. The rest of the team from position 5a moved forward to use the destroyed tanks as protection. The fighting was horrific, and the team did not even need to aim much, because the fighters were too numerous. The bombing continued wiping out vehicles and dozens of fighters with each shot.

In the rear of the fighting near lookout position 1, not all the vehicles and jeeps made it past that second bend. The fighters attempted to storm the positions but were met with stone barrels, followed by oil barrels, spewing slippery oil all over the rocks they were attempting to climb, followed by a barrel bomb, and finally followed by barrels with just gasoline. They set the hill on fire for a bit. This combination took out nearly one hundred fighters on every assault wave. The snipers fired at the barrel bombs and propane tanks in the area between positions 1 and 2 along the roadside, destroying dozens of fighters each time.

The team commenced dropping barrel bombs on those in the jeeps on the other side of the bend using the catapult and dropping a variety of the bombs, rocks, and oil. Every fourth round included a barrel of just gasoline, and this combination together created great destruction with the flying debris, setting much of the road on fire.

A dozen of the jeeps retreated, but Aaron's team had the sniper and the catapult focus upon those retreating and extended the range of where the barrel bombs were being dropped so that they would fall just in front of the lead jeep. They wiped out most of the jeeps, but three of them were able to drive just out of range.

Several fighters made it near the second defensive positions, but Pierre took ahold of the nail gun and shot eight of the fighters in the head with the nails. The nail gun was better than a regular, single-action sniper gun for close range. The fighting between Pierre's position 2 and Aaron's position 1 became intense. The fighters were firing everywhere because they could not determine where the defensemen were. The blasts singing gave an illusion that we were everywhere in the mountain, and because the barrel bombs came from multiple locations and came flying from over the hill from positions 4, 5a, and 6, as well as from positions 1, 2, and 3, they had no idea of the locations of the defensive positions beyond the first bend. These fighters were not well disciplined. Their officers were in the rear with the jeep and not able to properly command them. Confusion was massive among the fighters, and they just shot their rounds up the mountain, where no one was stationed. It was another turkey trot, and we were butchering them badly.

However, no matter how poorly we felt about killing them, we knew we had to stop them here before they moved north to kill other civilians. Each time a barrel bomb hit during the fighters, this took out one to two dozen fighters and a few trucks, with two machine gun operators in each truck. The armored vehicles near bend 1 attempted to ram the turned-over tanks and then the bus. When one of the armored vehicles hit the tank next to the cliff, something in the tank exploded in an easterly direction and blew the tank and two of the armored units off the cliff. The other armored vehicle was sitting above a water drain, and Rick told command center to blow that drain containing plastic explosive and the larger barrel bombs. Just as Rick counted down, "Three...two...one...," Rick moved the bus away just in time as they blew the drain, not only destroying the armored vehicle, but sending the vehicle flying in the air as well, falling upon two trucks and a dozen fighters. Rick's team members lobbed a dozen or so grenades, starting from the seventy-foot mark to the two-hundred-foot mark, to clear the fighters rushing forward near the bend.

While they were lobbing the grenades, position 2 lobbed a barrel of gasoline down the mountain near the base of the mountain next to the bend, and as one of the grenades exploded, it also ignited the gasoline and set the whole bend area on fire to the east of the tank. While the flames were high, the dozer and loader operators pushed the remaining tank over the embankment, down into the ravine.

They cleared all the debris and moved the bus back into position, thus enabling them to place the dozer at the back portion of the bus and the loader behind the bus. Just as they finished pushing the bus back into its defensive position, four of the pickup trucks with two machine gun operators on each truck started moving toward the bus, and the gun operators opened fire upon the bus. The steel sheeting and sandbags in the bus protected those in the bus. Rick radioed positions 2 and 6 to drop more barrel of gasoline near their position as they moved slowly forward, but they stopped where the flames were, and just then, the two barrel bombs landed in front of the truck and the second landed just in the back of them, shredding the trucks and fighters into pieces and killing everyone within a hundred feet.

Positions 4, 5, and 6 were now focusing on the central portion between defensive positions 1, 2, and 3, catapulting their barrel bombs toward the area near position 1 to keep the fighters from escaping. Rick's machine gun team was firing directly into the crowds of fighters, and they were being moved down.

The fighting continued for nearly three hours. The resistance ended, and a half-dozen fighters attempted to surrender, and again the same two sharpshooters just killed them. This did not go well with most of the team. We did not know what to do if we took prisoners but terminating people who had surrendered was not a good thing to do because they had dropped their guns and pulled out a white flag or handkerchief with their arms raised in the air. Rick's team and members from the other teams joined in the cleanup. The teams rounded up any guns, grenades, grenade launchers, ammunitions, machine guns, and so forth from the battlefield.

As Rick's team cleared the area, the dozer and loader operators pushed the debris and the burnt bodies over the embankment to the ravine below. Another team filled in the craters caused by the blasts with stones, sand, and gravel from the foot of the mountain. They also set additional detonation devices buried in the sand directly below additional barrel bombs. These had electronic detonators, and Josh set them to explode on command.

According to Captain Roger's team, three jeeps with high-ranking officers from the enemy fled the fight and returned to their encampment. This became a concern to Colonel John because now the enemy knew our defense tactics and where we were located. We had to repair a portion of the road at the first bend where the water and sewer pipes were, because they had been blown away by the blast. We repaired a portion of it by covering it up with the canvas and placed barrels of gasoline and our barrel bombs with electronic detonators underneath with one-inch rocks and sand. They were to blow it up when the next tank came into view at the first bend.

After the cleanup and replacing the barrels and detonation devices along the road pathway, Colonel John requested a special meeting at the command center. All those in charge of each defensive position had to attend the meeting. Two members of each defensive positions had to remain at the post.

Captain Roger and Joshua sent up three planes to observe any activity coming from the neighboring town, where the fighters were encamped. Josh was able to program one of the planes to go out nearly seven miles and to return to our location without using the controls until it came within a mile of our defensive positions. They kept constant vigilance over the area during our meeting. We opened the meeting with prayer and worship. There was a deep sense of the presence of the Lord felt, and many broke out in tongues for twenty minutes.

Michelle stood up and spoke. "The Lord says, 'My children, most of you are performing according to the detailed plan I have established. However, there are a few who have not obeyed and a couple who are enjoying the killing of people. Killing becomes murder when the heart is not right.' 'All people are Mine, and justice is Mine,' says the Lord. 'Those who enjoy taking the life of others will be punished at the appropriate time, and those who do not obey, believe, or think that their will should replace my will, they also will be dealt with at the appropriate time. Search your hearts and come back to me. Repent! Your largest trials are still ahead. Do not hate, do not take joy in your victories, but feel compassion for your enemies, love your enemies, resist temptations, bring forth in this village a new hope and a new love. The sons of Satan are regrouping and will be coming up with a new strategy, and then they will come at you with everything they can muster. You have embarrassed them before their peers, and their pride has surfaced so that you must be dealt with immediately and swiftly. Sleep tonight, for a strange twist will occur before noon tomorrow. Do not be fooled by their trickery. You need to separate the goats from the sheep, and you will succeed. Test the spirit and you will succeed. All that glitters are not gold, as we have been once foretold. Remember how they came here and do remember what a normal refugee family looks like. Be smart and think and trust in your foreign experiences. I will send My spirit of discernment upon the worship team. They will discern the goats from the sheep. Use the police station and mental health facility to intern the goats. Remember that I will always be with you. I will continue to strengthen you and take heart in the fact that I love you so much for the sacrifice you are enduring for this thankless generations. Be of good stead, be of good cheer, and be of great courage, for the Lord, your God, casts His mercies upon you during the darkest hours. The Holy Spirit will increase your faith and knowledge of Him and will increase the gifts to all of you. Repent for the errors of your ways and be of good courage and continued faith by trusting in Me and My Word. May My peace be with you, always, to the end of your time.'"

As soon as Michelle finished, Irene arose and spoke. "My dearly beloved, I thank you so much for resisting the sons of Satan, but do not let your heart grow weary, or let hatred enter your heart. Do not forsake Me, nor should you allow pride and anger to enter the store-room of your heart. Remember the parable of the farmer who sowed good seeds but an evil neighbor decided to sow weeds in his neighbors' field. Your adversaries have decided to sow weeds into your field tomorrow. Be leery and be cautious of the weeds. Do not gather the weeds to the storehouse but segregate them to be burned at the appropriate time. In a like manner, you need to separate the goats from the sheep. Remember how they train their fighters from their youth. Evil knows not an age. Evil knows not a gender or a race. Evil is taught, and when it sinks into the heart, it is difficult to pluck out. Only the love of My Son can uproot evil. So be cautious and discern right from wrong, good from evil, and put them to the test. My Spirit will give everyone a new gift, and those who speak in tongues, I give you a new language tonight and tomorrow to discern what you must do. I love you all, even those who are not fully obedient. You must repent and confess your evil ways and change your heart before it becomes bitter or evil. Some of you are now concerned of the former Muslims in your midst, but take heart that they are not your enemy, as you will see in the next two days. You must use them to help discern good from evil and the goats from the sheep. Design a process tomorrow morning of how you will accomplish this. My Spirit will place in your hearts and in the hearts of the Bosnians and in the hearts of those who have served in Afghanistan and Iraq as to how to accomplish this. After morning prayer, you must gather your resources and set up your facility to accomplish this. Tonight, you may all rest. My host of angels will stand guard over you during the night, and no one will come out of their village. You will be safe tonight. You will need the rest because you will fight your hardest battles over the next two day. First, a battle of the heart, and second, a battle of faith and courage."

At that, Irene sat down, and Pastor David, Father Jake, and Rabbi Maskil arose and talked among one another for a few seconds. Then Pastor Dave spoke on their behalf. He said, "This is what we've discerned. The enemy will change their tactics tomorrow to trick us. We do not know exactly what they plan, but we must keep in mind the parables spoken. We must go into the Word tonight and re-read those parables and ask the Lord to open our minds and our hearts. He has given us the tools of His Spirit and the gifts of the Holy Spirit. We need to identify what they are so that we can use them tomorrow. Keep your minds, hearts, and wills open. Let love conquer your hearts and repent of anything not of God within your hearts, especially pride, hatred, evil thoughts and deeds, and pleasure gained from murder. All peoples are God's children. Evil knows no boundary, nor does it rest in any one group. The next two days will be the test of our heart, mind, and will. Will each of us pass the test? Can we individually uproot the evil planted in our own hearts and only discern the evil planted in the hearts of others? Pray tonight after worship in your own earnest to seek the Lord's will and to receive the gifts of His Spirit, especially tongues, discernment, faith, peace, and joy. Be open to receive these gifts. Use the gifts or they will be taken away from you and given to others who already have many gifts but have used them on behalf of his Master, our Lord."

The worship team commenced praising with, "Spirit of the Living God, fall afresh on us," and then "Not by power, not by might, but by My Spirit, says the Lord." Rabbi Maskil gave us a Mosaic rabbinical blessing. After that, we all went to our respective stations and prayed quietly and fell asleep quickly. During the night, many of us had similar dreams as to what we needed to do, but we were not clear of what the enemy had planned for us.

We arose at the crack of dawn and most of us gathered at command center with two individuals remaining at each station and Captain Roger kept flying his drones. We prayed, praised God Yahweh, Jesus, and the Spirit for over an hour, with the loudspeakers being activated. We shared Communion, or, as some called it, the breaking of the bread.

Then after Communion, Irene got up and spoke. "The Lord knows that many of you have not put the pieces together, but you will when the sun is at its highest. The light bulb will come on, and each one who has been called must respond and execute what the Lord has told you last night and use the gift ort gifts given to you to fulfill the plan. The leadership will be given what to do, but the gifts you received last night, and this morning, will be needed to execute the plans. Praise the Lord, your God, and sing to Him in the tongue given to you by His Spirit, and to those given the gift of interpretation, do not be afraid to speak out what you heard. To those given the gift of discernment, test the heart of those who are about to come. The Spirit of the Lord will rest upon you, and you will know the hearts of men and you will know the heart of the good or the heart of the evil. Be observant! Use the gifts given at the appropriate time and use them wisely. Remain in love, peace, and joy, or evil will overtake you. There are still some who have not repented and have been deceived by your own pride and anger from the past. Repent before tomorrow, for tomorrow will be judgment day for all. Be of great courage and faith. Be of good stead and do not be deceived by the enemy or by your own heart. I will be with you, and My heavenly host will also watch over you today and tomorrow, especially.

Continue to love one another just as I have loved you. The soldiers will not come today or tomorrow, so do not be afraid and stand your ground. You are not fighting men, but principalities. My grace will be sufficient for you as you increase your faith." The worship team started to sing Hillsong's "Love Won't Let Me Down."

Pastor Dave gave us a blessing, and we broke for breakfast. We had not eaten much in the past thirty-six hours, and we were famished. The ladies and a few men prepared breakfast, and some of the men served the others. The leaders gathered to discern what the word meant. The issues raised were whether these were internal matters to individuals or the group, external situations, or a combination of both. They decided to pray over the matter and ask the Lord for clarification. After breakfast, Colonel John suggested each position do what they needed to do to refortify their specific defensive positions. Each defense leader was to take inventory of their remaining arsenal of ammunition, barrel bombs, propane tanks, barrels of oil, rock, and gasoline.

At around 8:30 a.m., the drone spotted activity coming out of the village. This time, there were over two thousand armed men, plus over five tanks, ten armored carriers, and fifty trucks of various sizes ascending the winding road toward our mountain pass. Leading the way were several trucks with soldiers manning machine guns, and they were lined up alongside of a group of individuals who appeared not to be soldiers. It looked like approximately two hundred civilians. There were trucks at the rear of this group that also had soldiers manning machine guns. The tanks and armored vehicles were in the rear of the convoy, which was totally different from prior attacks.

Captain Roger sent up additional drones and planes to get a better view of what was coming down the road. The convoy was approximately four miles away and coming toward us at about two miles per hour. The drones and the planes made several passes over and near the convoy. They returned via another route, but the last plane took a minor detour and flew over the non-soldiers walking in the front of the convoy. The plane took pictures and sent them to the command center and Colonel John, where the leadership looked at the pictures intently. As a matter of fact, they thought they could recognize two or three of the individuals in the pictures. Those leading the pack appeared to be civilians, and none of them held any weapons. Most of them appeared to be women, children, and some young men between the ages of sixteen and twenty-two years.

The thought process of the colonel was that he believed ISISA was going to use these individuals as human shield so that we would not explode the bombs. The leadership was going to decide as to what we would do if they did that. We knew that ISISA had done this so often in Iraq, and they had no scruples or morals. The decision was to wait and see what they would do.

It was now just past noon, and the convoy was now less than a mile away at the third bend in the road. It appeared that the back half of the convoy stopped. Captain Roger sent his drones and planes up again to survey the situation. Most of the soldiers, tanks, and other vehicles stopped at the one mile marker, but the trucks manned with the machine guns continued forward with the civilians. One jeep vehicle with three soldiers in it pulled in front of the civilians and now was carrying a white flag attached to a pole.

Colonel John summoned Captain Gary and Moe to the command center to discuss alternatives when they met the enemy. Captain Gary was holding his automatic rifle, and Moe carried a white flag and walked toward the second bend near defensive position 1 in view of the defensemen. Colonel John moved three additional sharpshooters to defensive position 1, and three snipers to position 2. They waited there for the group to come to their position. The jeep moved toward Captain Gary and Moe and stopped ten feet in front of them. One of the men sitting in the rear of the jeep disembarked from the jeep, and the other soldier sitting in the passenger seat with an automatic rifle also got out of the jeep and walked up to us with the other soldier.

Moe asked him, "Did you come to surrender?"

The soldiers laughed, and one said to us, "I am General Amid Al Mohammed Zadar from the new caliphate of North America. I came to offer you a temporary truce, and in exchange for that truce, I am freeing 160 prisoners. We have decided not to invade your territory. We will keep what we've conquered, and you can keep the rest of your land."

Moe asked him, "Are you telling me that there are only 160 survivors from a village of 35,000 residents? Did you kill the rest?"

The general answered, "We killed those who resisted or did not conform to our laws, but we still have several hundred prisoners, and many others were liberated and have joined our caliphate. We just wanted to offer you a token gesture of our sincere peace offering."

Moe asked, "Are you allowing these civilians to leave your caliphate? They are free to go?"

The general responded, "Yes, they all are free to go."

Moe then said, "Okay, General, you are free to go. Just have them sit down on the road and we will bring them water, and then we will take them in with us. We will wait until all your troops have left the area before we move the civilians."

Captain Gary said to General Zadar, "I do not believe you came in peace. We are not going to fight your battle—we will end your movement. I need to warn you that our God reigns and He will be fighting with His host of angels for us. Yahweh prospered this nation that worshipped and acknowledged Him. He will destroy those who turned their back on Him, and especially those who mark Him or His Son. Your caliphate is evil and is from Satan, and Yahweh, the God of Israel, will not allow this holy ground that Yahweh has consecrated in the name of His Son, Jesus, to be possessed by Satan. What will happen to you will be what Elisha the Tishbite did to Jezebel's priests. They were all destroyed, and I mean *all*."

At first, the general looked angry, but then he said something in Arabic then they mockingly laughed. Then the general and the soldiers turned around, got into the jeep, and headed back to the other trucks. They drove back to the location of the tanks, and everyone turned around and went back, heading south to the neighboring village.

Captain Gary radioed the command center, and they sent fifteen armed men to our area. Initially, we moved the civilians between defensive positions 1 and 2 but closer to bend 1. We had them sit down near the road again. Captain Gary cautioned Colonel John about the tricks they pulled on US troops in Iraq and Syria. ISIS would mingle their fighters with the refugees to infiltrate the defenses of the enemy or survey neighboring areas. The ladies came down with water and food for the civilians. While they were doing that, Rabbi Maskil came forward with Pastor Dave, Father Jake, and two of the ladies walked among the civilians. They told Colonel John, Captain Gary, and Moe what they discerned about what the Lord said and how it fit the current circumstance. They agreed on what Captain Gary had told the colonel. They discerned that this was a trick and we needed to ascertain who the enemy plants were.

Everyone went off to the side and prayed for a word of knowledge as to how to handle this situation. Irene came walking over to Moe and Rabbi and said to them, "I received a word from the Lord, and He said that we need to process the women and their children one at a time and talk to them separately. Those with Mideastern accents should also be further separated from any child over the age of twelve. The male children thirteen years or older, to the age of seventeen, should be separated from the other males eighteen and over. We sent the woman with one of the armed men to interview the women and female children first and to interview them separately from the group. We asked them their name, the spelling of their names, their age, date of birth, address, if they were citizens or when they came to this country, occupation of all parents, phone number, and social security number. We asked them if they were married and, if so, the name of their husband and children and the ages of their children. Another group interviewed the children under thirteen and asked them the same questions plus the name and spelling of their mothers' names. Another group interviewed the male children thirteen to seventeen, asking the same questions. After questioning all the civilians separately, we compared notes and found that several bits of information did not agree.

The condition of some of the women was very poor. Most of the women had been raped several times by the soldiers. Only about six of the women said the soldiers treated them very well. We also identified two other women as being elected officials. One was a US representative from the neighboring state, and she was the representative who sponsored the bill to open the borders of our country. She was a terrible wreck, severely beaten and abused by many of the soldiers. She was probably beaten badly because she was known to have an arrogant mouth and to be very verbose and demanding. In the Arab culture, women were to remain silent in the presence of a man in front of other men. We were sure she had a hard time with that. She could hardly talk, and they knocked out many of her teeth. She was black-and-blue all over. They had killed her husband and her children in front of her, according to Fran. She was broken and in despair.

After comparing notes, we took the women with minor female children under sixteen and male children under thirteen whose information matched in the separate interviews. We brought this group, ten or twelve at a time, to the high school locker room to shower, while a couple of ladies took their sizes and went to the clothing store and brought them appropriate clothes from the store that fit them. They brought them food and beverages and were asked to stay at the high school for further processing and transportation to the north.

The next group we processed were the males over thirteen but younger than eighteen. We had them interviewed by Father Jake, Pastor Dave, Rabbi Maskil, and a few of the men and women who felt the Holy Spirit had given them the gift of discernment. We divided them into two groups, those who were born in this country and those who came here within the past ten years. Those born in this country were interviewed first and then processed. Just before we were to bring this group to the high school, one of those discerning of spirits told us to look at the back of their hand or the back of their necks because they felt there was something strange about them. After inspecting them closely, Jack spotted two of the older boys had something behind their necks near their ears. We called in our computer IT persons, Josh and Gordon, to identify what this was. Gordon pretended he was a doctor, and Joshua brought an item that detected planted bugs, which came from Captain Roger's electronics store (Captain Roger had been in Army intelligence for four years). The pretend doctor did a few fake medical tests, and then

Joshua pulled out the detection device while giving him an eye test, and the device alarm went off.

The enemy planted a bug in the back of their young soldiers' necks near the ear so they could know their location and would be able to hear everything said near them. We sent some of our women to check out the women and children at the school, and they found nothing. We then had some of the women now check the other group of women and their children who had come to our country during the past ten years. Bingo—they found five of the women and three of their children with these devices implanted in the same place! We brought this group to the middle school with armed guards. After they showered, we gave them clothes and then brought them to the mental health clinic, which had locked and padded rooms. The ladies gave them all Bibles to read. While they were eating, Joshua's team wired the detention rooms and the jail so that we could hear what they were saying, and this was also wired to the command center.

We divided those between eighteen and twenty-five into two groups, American-born citizens and those who had been here for more than ten years versus those who had come to the US within the ten-year period. As we processed the two groups, we paid attention to the planted bug. We brought in armed guards, and then we brought in the bug detector. We had the civilians sit down in chairs, all in a row. While our fake doctor, Jim (he really was an EMT), came in and pretended to perform tests, Joshua went behind them with the detector. Of the forty-four men, the detector went off twelve times. We separated the twelve from the other thirty-two. We processed the thirty-two, and those with discernment okayed them to be processed at the high school. We took the twelve to the middle school to shower and brought them some very colorful clothes. The others had tan-, white-, or dark-colored clothing. We brought them to the village jail and locked them in. We then fed them and told them this was just temporary. From the police station, we were able to have someone verify the information supplied to us, and the only errors were those in the jail and those in the mental wards. We brought back one of the EMTs to the jail, and we took one of the prisoners to the local clinic, injected him, and he went under. We removed the device so that we could test it. Captain Roger and Gordon ran some diagnostics. It confirmed our suspicion: it had GPS capabilities, and it also had a chip that would transmit voices. While the men were at the middle school, Joshua and his team also wired the jail so that we could hear the men talking, and this allowed what they were saying to be also transmitted to command center. One of the Iraqi counter-intelligence vets, Bret, also spoke and understood Arabic and Farsi.

We praised the Lord for the information He foretold. The enemy did attempt to infiltrate our ranks and monitor our activity. We brought some chains and locks and locked certain interior rooms to contain the civilians, and then we locked all the exterior doors to make sure our guests would stay in the building assigned.

We assigned two of the women and two men from the service team to oversee all our guests, to be sure they were fed and were given water. They brought the men in the jail some bacon and eggs, and they all refused to eat the bacon. This also helped confirm our suspicion.

Meanwhile, at the command center, we had Bret, who had served in Iraq and Afghanistan, listen to the communications of our two groups of guests. Some of the women with children and all the men started to talk in Arabic after we left the facility. They thought they had fooled us, and they were planning on how they would pretend to assist us in the fighting and how they would be able to get the guns to kill us. We expected the young men to volunteer to help fight the ISISA forces, and then once they did so, they would turn against us according to the general's plan. We kind of played along as if we were considering this. We told everyone not to let any of these refugees know how many we were or our other defensive positions. This was a definite confirmation that we were right. We taught the caretakers to keep stringing them on about the temporary basis, until the soldiers brought in reinforcement tomorrow. Then they would take them north to the refugee camps. They were not happy campers when they heard the Army was coming with reinforcement tomorrow. They were talking about this so that the enemy would make their move before the soldiers came. As we thought, one of the older young men approached one of the guards in the jail and acted as if he wanted revenge and he and several of the young men wanted to stay and fight with us. We continued to let them believe that they would be assisting us after the soldiers came to assist us in the next big defensive move. They asked how many fighters were coming and how many we had now. The jail keeper told them we had fifteen hundred fighters and twenty thousand fighters were arriving tomorrow morning.

After the guards left, we could hear them talking loudly in Arabic so that the transmitters would send the information back to the command center. We heard them say that the soldiers were coming tomorrow to reinforce the pass and that they would be allowed to fight. They said that they would try to get assigned to the first two defensive positions to allow the ISISA fighters to advance to defensive position 3 very easily. We also heard them telling them about the defensive positions they had walked through to get to the village. We heard them describing the catapults, number of barrels, piles of rocks, storage sheds, and other information of what we had along the route.

This information was forwarded to Colonel John and the leadership. They looked at the plan and, as a result of the recent information, now understood what needed to be done. They discussed the details of the plan based upon what needed to be done and how we were to trick the spies into believing they would assist us in defending the positions. Then Colonel John decided to remove all the remaining bomb and gasoline barrels except two from position 1. The two barrels were remotely wired with plastic explosives, and the barrels were hidden among the barrels of rocks.

We also dismantled the catapult and reassembled it at defensive position 5c on the north side of the mountain pass. Colonel John called Captain Mark and updated him on what the status was. The colonel started off by saying, "Captain Mark, this is Colonel John. We have rescued approximately one hundred forty civilians and have taken twenty prisoners. So far, we do not have any casualties, and we have destroyed over twelve tanks, twenty armored vehicles, ninety trucks, and have killed over four thousand fighters. So you said you would be here in three days. Today is day 5, and you are missing out on all the fun. We were told by the prisoners that they are amassing an all-out assault with over six thousand troops, fifty tanks, a hundred fifty armored vehicles, and four hundred trucks. So do you want us to handle it by ourselves, or would you like to join us?"

Captain Mark responded, "I know I told you we would be back in three days, but we have not fully regrouped or reorganized. We will be there in two more days. What I can do for you is remove the refugees right away and take the prisoners off your hands at the same time. We will send five buses, three for refugees and two for the prisoners. They will be accompanied by four platoons of armed soldiers, one platoon for the refugees and three platoons for the prisoners. They will be dispatched in twenty minutes, and they will be there within two hours."

The colonel also told Captain Mark that we discovered several of the prisoners had transmitters implanted in the back of their necks. We had been playing them and letting them believe that they were playing us. They had been communicating back to their command center just by talking in Arabic about everything they had seen, and they had been asking to assist us in defending the pass. They believed that we had fifteen hundred defenders and kept asking which unit we belonged to and how many defensive positions we had. We had told them nothing except lies and exaggerations. We had told them that we had killed over four thousand of the enemy's fighters. We had told them our troops could easily wipe out two or three thousand more fighters.

Captain Mark said, "That was not the thing to say. Next time they will advance with everything they have. They are just stalling until all their troops are assembled, and your next battle will be your last battle. If you truly have killed four thousand fighters, that means they will attack you with five to six thousand men and many tanks and armored vehicles. They also have mortar equipment and at least one or two airplanes they have captured at the last airport."

The colonel asked, "When you send down your four platoons, can you send down more guns, ammunition, rocket-propelled grenade launchers, flamethrowers, and anything else you can spare?" Captain Mark said that he would talk to the general, but right then they did not even have enough for their own troops, so it would be very doubtful.

Captain Mark said, "I hope what you have told me is true about the four thousand! I will report that to the general, but he will not believe that seventy men could have wiped out all those people and equipment."

Colonel John immediately responded, "No, not seventy men. Fifty-eight men and twelve women with the help of the heavenly host and our Creator, to be exact. Yes, the four thousand is true, and if you come down here, you can smell them—the ravine stinks badly. We feel that there will be one last battle, and either we will wipe them out or they will take the pass with great casualties. We will stand our ground to the last person. It is not our battle, but the Lord's, and it is His victory, not ours."

"Please caution your men about the prisoners. Let them believe that they will be trained to assist in the fighting, until you have had a chance to remove those devices in the back of their necks, because whatever you say will be heard by the enemy."

Captain Mark said to the colonel, "If what you have told me is true, no one will ever believe what has taken place. We are not ready to confront the fighters, because our division has not fully been assembled, nor do we have the adequate firepower to do our job. We are awaiting helicopters from Canada. I pray that your God continue to be with you and your volunteers."

Two hours went by and no one showed up. Three, four, five hours, and still no one from Captain Mark's unit came to pick up the refugees. Colonel John called Captain Mark back and asked, "Where are your men who were going to pick up the refugees and prisoners? I forgot to tell you that one of the refugees is a US representative."

Captain Mark responded by saying, "The general overruled me and told me he could not spare anyone, nor did they have a facility for prisoners."

The colonel asked, "Then why did you not call me back?"

Captain Mark said, "Orders!"

Colonel John said, "Therefore, we are on our own, and we will just stand our ground and let the Lord have the victory. I am not surprised, because this has been already foretold." At that, Colonel John just hung up the phone and called his team to get together at sunset for praise, worship, and a meeting.

We fed the refuges and prisoners first, and then we ate a steak dinner with plenty of other great things that the service team of women and the chefs had prepared. One of the Vietnam soldiers satirically commented, "This seems like the last supper!" We did not take too kindly about that statement, but Pastor Dave said, "No, that will be after the praise-and-worship part of our service." He was referring to Communion.

At sunset, most of us gathered at the command center, except two individuals at each defensive position numbers 1, 2, and 6. We opened with a blessing, a prayer, and then started the praise and worship. We put our loudspeakers up full blast so that the enemy would hear it, as well as the refugees and prisoners. We praised for over an hour, thanking the Lord for all He had done and that all the glory, honor, and praise be to Yahweh and Jesus, His Son. We went into the worship portion, and everything was just so solemn, and peace fell upon us. Many broke out in tongues, and it was like the heavenly host was with us in worship. This lasted for another hour, and then we went into silent personal-prayer mode for another twenty minutes.

Irene and Estelle both went up and, one after another, almost in harmony, spoke. "I am pleased with you, and tomorrow, you will be confronted by more than six thousand fighters that will come upon you at once. You need to focus upon the pass, for they will commence their bombardment with mortar rounds from the ravine. Fear not, for I will be with you. I have summoned Michael and the heavenly host to assist you in this major battle. The bombs will explode in the air and will not do any harm to any of the seventy. They will attempt to scale the mountain walls, but when they do, you will need to blow the walls as directed. First, the lower walls, and then the upper walls of the mountain. You must wait until one fighter reaches the top of each wall. The soldiers will mount wave after wave of assaults, but you will be victorious. The bodies will be stacked so high that in the end they will have to climb over the bodies to get to you. You must give up and retreat defensive positions 5a and 5b and then stand your ground at position 5c. When you retreat from each position, you will need to blow everything up upon getting back to the other fallback defensive positions. The fight will be fierce, and you will need to retrench position 6 and bring your people to position 5. Bring your male prisoners to position 1, and when the fighters come and reach position 2, you will need to blow the two mountain walls and position 1 totally. Give them rifles that will jam upon firing the first round and remove our people. The enemy will not attack position 6. They will concentrate on the pass, and they will order their troops to advance or be shot by the fighters behind them. They are amassing their troops and will attack at dawn. Bring the male prisoners to position 1 twenty minutes before dawn.

"Know that you are My people, and I am your God. Fear not. Be of great courage. For it is written in David's Psalm 28:7 that I, your Lord, am your strength and shield. Most of you have served Me well, but I will remove My protective hand from four of you, lest they repent. I tell you this so that the rest of you should be alarmed. They have not repented, nor have they cleansed their heart from the evil they have done. Blessed is the one who repents as the thief on the cross. Your fame will not be of this world, but you will not share the glory of your deeds. You will be remembered for a while, then you will be forgotten. My Father will remember you for all eternity and esteem you as He does the twenty-four.

"Now go, rest, and reassemble at four tomorrow morning. Tomorrow will go down as one of the greatest modern battles before Armageddon. Then the world will know that I am God, and you are My people. I am in control of all the elements and I will leave My mark for all to see."

Irene and Estelle sat down.

Michelle arose and spoke. "I will pour out My anointing upon you. You may not substitute your own created anointing for My anointing. Any anointing from the flesh will perish. There is no substitute for the anointing by My Holy Spirit. Be careful not to substitute yours instead of that of My Spirit. I am Jehovah Jireh, your protector. I will pour out My grace upon you, which will increase your faith, your joy, and your courage. Real faith requires action and obedience to My commands and Word." Then she sat down in silent prayer.

After ten minutes of silence, Colonel John spoke. "I have talked to Captain Mark, and all he has told us was, he is under orders and cannot help us at this time. They are not ready to fight the enemy, and they need a few more days to be battle-ready. Their supplies and troops are almost assembled. We and our God are all that is between the enemy and the people up north. We must stand our ground and defend this pass. God is with us, so who can be against us? We need to dig down deeply into all our faith and trust the Lord. Be of great courage and fear not."

Captain Gary spoke. "You heard the Lord tell us that the enemy will be throwing everything they have at us tomorrow. The last battles involved less than two thousand fighters, and the fighting was difficult, but this time the enemy knows some of our strategies and we will need to follow the Lord's plans to a tee, or, should Rabbi say, the last *tittle*. This time we will have Michael and his heavenly host assisting in our defense. Our service teams will bring you whatever food during the battle. Expect it to last all day. No one should leave his post until the designated time. Keep your eyes on the cross and listen to the Word of God through the praise-and-worship songs. Meditate upon the Word. Listen to the whispers of God's voice and follow them. We will light up the crosses starting at midnight. Expect the battle to be a lengthy one, but God will strengthen us for those who place their faith in the Lord, our Savior. Again, I say, we need to follow the plan our Lord has given us."

The colonel went over the plans position by position for all to hear and know. Colonel John said, "We will transfer the team from position 1 to position 2 and between position 3 under the command of Pierre. Those in position 6 need to go to position 5 under the command of Rick. These are in accordance with God's word." We needed to set up the fake defensive position between 5b and 5c with the soldier mannequins and other traps. They were removed prior to bringing the enemy captives in the jail. They believed we had four pass defensive positions. This would fall right into the plan. We were ordered to remove much of the supplies to the final defensive position.

After that, the colonel dismissed everyone to their posts to get some sleep. They brought two days' provision of water and protein snacks. We did not know how long the battle would be. Some of us were concerned as to who the "four" were from which the Lord was removing His protective hand and hoping, or should I say praying, it was not them. A few thought that the two rebellious vets would be among them, but they were at their post when the word was given. We hoped they hear the message and prayed that they would repent before tomorrow morning.

Several of us went back to assist Tom and George make more bullets. We worked about another two hours and realized that we just ran out of powder and other materials. We knew based upon the word that the battle would now focus upon the pass and that Tom and Rick's team would need the bulk of what we made, so Tom and Rick took what we made that night back to position on the northern and last defensive position at the pass.

A number of others went back to the various stores and picked up numerous other items, like hammers, hatchet, arrows, spears, hoes, lanterns, knives, racks, metal and wooden objects to throw, glass and plastic containers, and anything else that could be thrown or used as a weapon. They brought them to positions 4 and 3.

The rest of us went back to our designated areas to rest because we knew we needed to get up early because tomorrow would be the longest day of our lives.

W e went to sleep and awoke at three fifteen in the morning. We knew that the soldiers were not coming as promised, as Yahweh had foretold. We prepared our sites, and those in defensive position 1 went down to the jail and awoke the prisoners. We told them that they passed the test and they were accepted as fighters and they would assist in defending one of the positions. They asked to separate, and each of them would assist in defending other positions as well. The guard told them that he would bring it to the commander's attention, but they all needed to go to the initial assigned position, and some would be transferred to other defensive positions, and someone would bring them weapons at that time. They were smiling, thinking they had deceived us again, but we did not let them know what the real facts were. We transported them to the upper level of position 1, where the men at the post told them they had cooked breakfast for them and told them to sit down and eat for it was going to be a long day. Our team said they were going to get the rest of the guns and ammunition and bring them back before sunrise. The service team had prepared lots of food for them, and when sunrise came, they looked out and rejoiced when they saw their troops coming down the road. One of our last members stayed there, saying, "I will go down to find the others who were getting the guns and ammunition." The two guns they had been given had blanks in the clip.

As he departed, he returned to the command center, and Captain Roger had already sent up his drones and his planes. He was monitoring the advancing troops and position 1 with the surveillance cameras. They had already told their ISSA commander they were the only defensemen at the upper level of position 1. As the fighters came forward to the second bend, some of the fighters commenced climbing the east side of the mountain. As they went up the mountain wall, the troops continued to march forward. This time the tanks and armored vehicles were not in the front of the convoy but toward the rear of the brigade. The columns of fighters now commenced running toward bend 1 and our defensive position 2 and 5a. There were soldiers for over two miles and dozens of tanks, armored vehicles, trucks, and jeeps and pickup trucks. Captain Roger told Colonel John, "They are throwing all they have this time at us. There are over six thousand troops parading down the road from Zoar. Get everyone ready. I am sending a drone near the upper level of position 1, and we will need to do something real soon."

Captain Roger, Josh, Gordon, and the rest of the communications team were able to get a dozen of lavaliers working and connected to the speakers and monitors so that some of the ladies could assist the men in positions 3 and 4. Irene, Michelle, and two of the Bosnian women especially requested this so that they could be with their husbands in what we all perceived to be the final battle.

Looking out at the enemy troops, most of our people perceived it was impossible for seventy people to defend against over six thousand hardened troops without divine intervention. Several perceived that although we might hold the pass until Captain Mark returned, majority would be sacrificed in the process. They did not pay attention to what the Lord had said. So the ladies thought, if their husband was going to be one of the four, they wanted to die fighting with their husbands up to the last minute while singing Yahushua's praise. The communications team retrofitted Irene, Michelle, Fran, Ishmarta (Niaz's wife), Zefina (Sejad's wife), Diane, Estelle, and three other ladies with the lavaliers so that they could still sing with the praise group yet be with their spouse during this next battle to assist them in reloading the bullets into the clips or whatever else was needed.

The praise teams started singing songs of faith and songs of God's glory and might. They cranked up the loudspeakers for all to hear. They started to sing, "Nothing Can Stop the Unstoppable God, Where Does My Help Come From?" followed by "My Fear Does Not Stand a Chance When I Stand in Your Love" and "Jesus Is the Center of It All."

We waited until many of the fighters had reached halfway to the first bend, past the second bend, where the fighters commenced attacking with great vigor; then Lieutenant Bernie, under the direction of Captain Roger, blew up the upper level of position 1 when the first of the fighters reached the designated mark near position 1 and, immediately thereafter, blew up the first lower wall of the south-side east mountainside, which was over five hundred feet long around the first defensive position, which sent all those spies into the air as well as those climbing the mountain on the east and west side of that position. The blowing up of the lower mountain wall sent thousands of tons of granite stone raining down for over a thousand feet, plus the initial blast blew everyone next to the wall and cliff for five hundred feet into the air and over the cliff into the ravine. This took out a couple hundred fighters, jeeps, and trucks also.

The men in the lower level of defensive position 1 sought shelter in the metal containers just before the blast. They had been warned by Captain Roger's team a minute before.

The enemy commenced firing the mortars, but just as the Lord said, the mortar just blew up in the air like fireworks. As a matter of fact, many of the mortars and shell fragments were even hitting their own fighters, caused by blowing up some of their vehicles and the troops behind them. It was like the angels were playing baseball practice, and many of the rounds were flying back to where they came from, taking out some of the mortar positions. A few of the tanks fired their rounds, but only about a little more than a half-dozen rounds went way beyond the mountain into the areas of the fields, and possibly near the homes just outside the village.

When the first explosion occurred, all the teams from defensive position 2 to defensive position 5 opened fire at the barrel bombs, gasoline barrels, rocks, and everything available. Before position 6 closed, we had brought all their remaining items to positions 2 through 5 the previous night and early morning. Positions 2, 3, and

4 concentrated their catapults onto the portion of the mountain between the first two bends, while position 5 focused upon those fighters coming down the road near the first bend. The fighters just kept on coming and coming, and the machine guns were mowing them down by the dozens, and the barrel bombs would take out fifty to sixty at a time.

Initially, half of position 3 was helping position 2, and the other half, except for those manning the catapults, assisted in defending the pass. Position 4, except for the person manning the catapult, was involved with defending the pass, but those manning the catapults were focusing on sending their barrel bombs to the area between the two bends. The snipers, marksmen, and sharpshooters from position 1 were assisting position 2 and shooting at the barrel bombs just as they were about ten to twenty feet above the fighters' heads, taking out three to five dozen fighters at a time. They just kept on coming and coming. The fighters charged down the portion of the road just after the first bend. As they came over the first group of barriers near the bend halfway between the first bend and position 5a, Captain Roger and Lieutenant Bernie blew up some of the barrels and detonated the hidden barrels and plastic explosives buried in the roadside and in the sewer and water drains, taking out three tanks and over a hundred of the fighters, sending them into the air and some over the cliff. Yet they kept coming and coming down the road. They were like ants in a sugar patch. They were so vicious and determined. The general must have threatened them because they did not care if they lived or died. They were on a jihad mission.

When hundreds of fighters were approximately fifty feet away, Rick's team opened the machine guns and just kept firing and firing, while Vinko's and Jasmine's teams were firing the catapults and concentrating near the bend, taking out those rounding the bend and a hundred feet north of the bend. They would sequence the firing with rocks first, barrel bombs second, and the gasoline barrels third and begin the firing sequence again and again. This intense fighting went on for nearly two hours, yet the fighters kept on coming and coming.

The bodies were piling up, and the enemy had to jump over the burnt dead bodies of their own fighters. A few fighters attempted to retreat, only to be shot by their own fighters.

Back at the second bend, where defensive position 1 was located, hundreds of fighters were killed by the blast. The tanks were stuck behind all that rock in the roadway. Their commanding officer ordered the tanks to go over the rocks and assist their fighters. As the tanks proceeded one after another, and when there were twenty tanks on the rocks between position 1 and the area west for nearly five hundred feet, Captain Roger's drone saw them and then ordered the demolition team to blow the second layer of the mountain explosives for the ledge eighty feet above the tanks. When the mountain ledge exploded, hundreds of thousands of tons of rocks were sent for a thousand feet, and the blast itself was so powerful that between the effects of the blast and the tons of rocks, eighteen of the tanks were blown over the cliff and down into the ravine seven hundred feet below. In addition, over two hundred of their fighters walking alongside the tanks were also destroyed. Now the rock piles in the road area were even higher, yet their general ordered another twenty tanks and armored vehicles to proceed. The tanks had to climb twice as high over the rocks, and some of the tanks and vehicles tipped over and went down the ravine. Others blocked most of the way for the remaining tanks and vehicles, and they could not proceed any farther. The general ordered the fighters to proceed despite the obstacles. None of the trucks could pass beyond the rocks, so the general, who was now incensed, ordered the fighters in the trucks and tanks to take their rifles and machine guns and go at it on foot.

At the first bend and the second defensive position, everyone had their hands full, and the shooters kept blowing up the barrels and propane tanks planted, and those being flung into the air by the catapults. Their focus was upon the positions between the two bends, especially from the blast area to the first bend, plus just below the first bend. The team dropped barrels of gasoline onto the fighters below, and then they would throw a grenade, which set them on fire, blowing up many. Our teams just kept fighting. The stench of burning flesh permeated the air initially, but the Lord sent a breeze from the north and the west, which sent the smell away from our area, toward the advancing fighters.

Defensive position 5a started to run out of ammunition at that location, and Rick ordered his team back to position 5b, where other weapons and ammunition awaited them. Systematically, they retreated by way of the hidden sewer pipes. Just as Rick got through to his position, the fighters started to overrun position 5a. Just as they did, Rick blew the pipes and then detonated the previous defensive position with about fifty fighters there. Everyone and everything in that area was destroyed, which sent debris up in the air for a hundred feet, and the debris fell upon the other fighters. Now Rick's team was defending position 5b, located at the mouth of the southern portion of the pass. Vinko's team was sending rocks, barrels, and containers down the road areas. Two of Vinko's team members manning the catapults at defensive position 5b were still focusing on the bend, while three teams at defensive position 5c were focusing upon the area between the bend and position 5a.

Now, team members from position 3, command center, and those along the area between positions 4, 3, and 2 were also focusing on the area in front of positions 5a and 2. They were sending barrels of gasoline, rocks, and barrel bombs down a slide unto the fighters, which the shooters from position 4 would shoot the marked barrels and they would explode, taking out dozens of fighters at a time. Sharpshooters from position 3 would shoot at the barrels being dropped by position 4, plus the barrels sent up by Vinko's teams.

The battles raged on for an additional five hours. The men kept coming and coming. Thousands had already been destroyed, and over three dozen tanks, yet the enemy kept on coming. Most of the remaining tanks were stalled on the rocks, but six tanks made it through the second bend and now were heading for the first bend. They fired at defensive position 2, but their shells hit about forty feet below the defensive position, and the rocks blew off the mountain, only to hit their own soldiers.

Just as the sixth tank came off the rocks, Captain Roger and Bernie's detonation team was given the order to blow the second round of rocks about five hundred feet near the first bend in the road and seven hundred feet toward the second bend. They detonated the rocks about forty feet on the first lower ledge, just like a gravel pit blast, which took out everything for seven hundred feet between the first bend and everything seven hundred feet west of that bend. The blast was so immense that all the six tanks and most the fighters in that seven hundred feet were just blown off the mountain road down into the ravine.

Yet the general was still incensed and ordered the remainder of the tanks and armored vehicles to move forward over the rocks and debris. All the remaining soldiers were now between the two bends, slowly moving forward over the rocks and rounding the bend toward the mountain pass. On the road near the mountain pass, dozens of soldiers started to climb the mountain near positions 2, 3, and 4, while the fighters kept pouring toward position 5b at the southerly mouth of the pass. The bodies kept piling up. As the fighter continued to scale the mountain ledge between the west of positions 2 and 3, as well as the south and west wall of position 4, their bodies would fall into the pass between positions 5a and 5b.

There were so many fighters for which Rick's team needed to abandon position 5b and drop back to position 5c. As he directed Vinko's team to drop three barrel bombs five hundred feet away from his position, he ordered his team to start filing through the sewer pipes. He started with those in the V-shaped water pipes, and they took their weapons and remaining ammunitions with them. As Rick was awaiting one of the sharpshooters who hung back, Joe, formerly from defensive position 2, had hung back well beyond the required time, and as Joe now moved toward the pipes, and as he reached the entrance of the pipe, the fighters were just going over the defensive position 5b and one of the fighters shot Joe in the back and he fell at the entrance of the pipe. Rick heard Joe cry out as he was about to hit the ground, "Lord, forgive me for not obeying!" Rick quickly went back, lobbed a grenade near the entrance of the pipe, pulled Joe through the pipe, slashing the sandbags, which dropped the sand into the pipes to cover his escape route. When Rick reached the other side with Joe, he quickly pulled the lever and detonated the explosives in the pipes and throughout position 5b. The fighters who had just overrun position 5b were just making it onto the pass through the mountains when the detonation went off and at least two hundred more soldiers were blown away, with body parts flying in the air. Everything in position 2, including the containers, barrels, rocks, and barriers, was sent flying into the air toward the south, wiping out everything in its path.

The fighters kept on coming. As they poured through past position 5b, they started attacking the fake defensive position. By now, Rick's team was set up in position 5c, awaiting the fighters to pass the fake defensive position. As they began to overrun the position, the fighters started shooting the mannequins, and as they did, it exploded and took out several fighters. When other fighters pulled out the Israeli and American flags, this, too, set off the detonation devices and took out dozens more fighters by exploding the grenades attached to the barrel bombs.

Rick radioed positions 3 and 4 to now assist in defending the pass. There were no more positions to retreat to. Now it was do or die. He notified the command center that he just took on his first casualty, Joe. Now the fighters were storming through the pass, and many were continuing to climb the mountain to the fortified positions 2, 3, and 4. Some the fighters made it upon the first level of the mountain to the southern face of the lower level for positions 2 and 4 and the west wall of positions 2 and 3. Colonel John ordered Captain Roger and the detonation crew to blow the southern face of level 1 for the positions first, and then the west walls. Captain Roger hollered out, "Fire in the hole!" and everybody ducked. Rocks were flying everywhere. Not only were the fighters on the level and climbing the mountain blown away; it also took out nearly a hundred other fighters between the bend and positions 5a and 5b. The fighters kept on coming. We must have already taken out more than three thousand soldiers by now, but they were like ants, who just kept on coming.

Now we had our defensive positions fully activated in position 5c. Position 2 was no longer focusing upon the road between positions 1 and 2; it was focusing upon the fighters climbing the mountain, attempting to overtake position 2. Level 1 had been blown away, and Pierre was reluctant to blow away level 2. He and Normand were still dropping gasoline bombs in the area of those climbing the ledges. Now there were many soldiers about to reach the top of ledge 2, and Pierre called to Captain Roger to blow away all of ledge 2 positioned east and west of position 2 on the easterly mountain. As they were about to blow that portion, half a dozen fighters made it to the top of the ledge and started shooting, and Normand was hit in the head and was killed. Just as he fell back, Captain Roger loudly radioed out, "Fire in the hole!" and everyone ducked, and a mighty blast took out all those fighters on level 2, those climbing up to reach mountain defense 2, and those in the roadway below. This had such an impact that nearly two hundred fighters were sent flying due to the impact of the blast and the flying granite rocks. Rene and Jim, the paramedic, rushed and pulled Normand into one of the containers and verified to command center that our second warrior was taken down trying to defend position 2. Yet they just kept coming.

At defensive position 4, Moe's team, and now Lou's team, was defending the southern portion of the position, and Captain Gary's team was now defending the western side of the mountain pass below. The catapults were still dropping the barrels on the area after the bend between the first bend and position 5b. Yet the fighters just kept on coming. They were dropping two of the rock barrels first, then the barrel bombs, and lastly the gasoline bombs. They had moved some of the barrels from the catapult area to the ledge bordering the pass and commenced dropping both types of barrels onto the fighters below using slides and seesaws. They were also tossing eight-inch-minus rocks onto the fighters below. At the sixth hour, the pass was now loaded with dead bodies being burnt up from gasoline from the barrels. Some of our men ran out of ammunition and now were using the nail guns and bows and arrows to shoot with. They had sent most of the spare ammunitions to Rick's team, and only the sharpshooters and snipers had ammunition by this eighth hour of fighting. They were remarkably effective and did as much damage yet attempted to spare the bullets. It was after three in the afternoon, and most of us were pumped by the Spirit. The praise team singing songs containing scriptures helped the fighters retain their focus. They were singing "There's No God Like Jehovah" and "Our God Reigns."

When the fighting became intense, Michelle and Irene turned on the lights for the crosses so we could keep our focus on the cross and why we were here fighting. Jesus gave His life for us, and now it was our turn to sacrifice ourselves for the cross though obedience. After all, wasn't this what our church prayed for, "to be used mightily by God"? I remembered one member of the church saying, "Be careful of how you pray and what you pray for! You might just get what you ask for, but not what you expected."

Moe and his team were losing ground; so many fighters had started coming over the ledge that Moe called in to Captain Roger and Lieutenant Bernie to blow the south side of the upper ledge of defensive position 4, and Moe ordered his team to drop back and take cover behind the containers. As Moe was attempting to retreat, Captain Gary came out of nowhere and swung just past Moe. He had hooked up two nylon ropes to the crane and to the metal piece attached to the cross and came swinging around alongside the top of the defense ridge and knocked off three of the fighters coming over the top of ledge of the defense wall. Captain Gary landed near one of the containers and went into the container to take cover.

Three of the Bosnian men, Niaz, Sade, and Ruffard, had fastened a metal wire to two of their arrows and fired the arrows simultaneously, and the wire struck at least six of the fighters as they came over the ledge of the wall and sent them to their death below.

While Captain Roger's detonation team was identifying which charge it was, a dozen of the fighters made it to the ledge of the defensive position. One of them shot toward Moe, but Jack dived in front of Moe to protect him. He was in the back, and another round hit Moe in the chest, and they both went down together.

Irene saw her husband go down from the monitor in their home. She ran out of the room onto the staging area, where Moe was, and grabbed herself a baseball bat near the containers. As one of the remaining fighters was about to walk over to Jack and Moe to finish them off, Irene came from the west of him, shouting at him, "You son of Satan, in the name of Jesus, you will not do that and you shall be sent to the fiery pit of hell!" In a split second later, she hit him with the bat and he went flying over the ledge down eighty feet to his death. The other fighters just stood there stunned, because a Muslim killed by a woman would not go to his reward. This gave Niaz and Ruffard time to shoot several of the fighters with arrows, using a crossbow, while Sade ran to assist Irene and to drag Moe and Jack behind the containers. As Irene wept, they called Rene, the paramedic, to assist Moe and Jack. Jack was dead. When Rene made it to Moe, he was looking for the blood and found none. The bullet hit Moe in the chest, right where his pocket-size New Testament book was located, and the blow of the bullet just knocked the wind out of him and knocked Moe unconscious.

When Rene took the bullet out of his New Testament, and when they removed the bullet, which was at the page in the book where the bullet stopped, it pointed to the passage, "You shall not die but shall have everlasting life." Rene revived Moe, and Irene's tears of sadness turned into tears of joy.

Lieutenant Bernie finally detonated the south ledge in front of defensive position 4. This blast took out another hundred or so soldiers easily. The rest of the team came out of the containers and went back to the ledge defensive positions. Moe got up and took his position at the point of the wall, and Irene went back to her position, praising the Lord with greater vigor. The rest of the team went back to the ledge defensive positions along the pass.

Meanwhile, Rick's team members below were still having a tough time. As they shot one person, two more showed up. Rick's team commenced firing the old Civil War cannon. They loaded it with a cannonball and two coffee containers filled with ball bearings and screws. When the fighters were fifty feet away, they would fire the cannon and it would take out nearly everyone within a hundred feet, because the metal was like a big buckshot spraying the area with metal.

Vinko and Jasmin brought forward the two whale harpoons that had been in the museum and placed them eighty feet apart. They tied a steel wire to the harpoon spears and ignited them. The spears flew shoulder high just as about fifty fighters were twenty feet away. As the metal wire tightened, it decapitated all those rushing the defensive position. They reloaded just in time for the next wave of attackers, and again, with the same results, the fighters dropped without their heads. They did this for a third time, and with the same results. The ISISA fighters saw all hundred or so bodies lying in front of them without heads, so they came to a halt about fifty feet away from the defensive position.

Every position was running out of ammunition and barrels and was resorting to nail guns, bows, arrows, javelins, sledgehammers, rocks, bowling balls, hammers, and crowbars, or whatever else was left from the containers. The Bobcats were pushing all the remaining rocks, blocks, barricades, and even some containers from positions 2, 3, and 4 onto the fighters below at the pass. All available personnel and teams, including the medics, food servers, and several of the women, were throwing rocks and whatever they could get their hands on over the ledge down toward the fighters.

The fighters were now pouring into the pass, and the ISISA general could taste victory. Now all the rest of his men were in the pass. There still were over fifteen hundred soldiers in the pass now moving to the last defensive position. They seemed to have focused upon the crosses behind the northerly defensive position and the crosses where George's and Irene's mountain homes were. The sight of the crosses infuriated them into a wild rage, like a cat smelling catnip. They would charge aimlessly about, with no true sense of direction, and their anger raged within.

Then, Captain Roger's drone spotted two small commercial planes coming toward Captain Gary and Moe's defensive position 4, and it swooped down on the first pass to assess the activity. On the second pass, they swooped down again, but this time both planes commenced firing upon their positions. Then Rabbi Maskil had a word of knowledge and told Colonel John to cut the tarp ropes and expose the mirrors. The mirrors were facing the west, and the planes were coming from the west. It was now four o'clock in the afternoon; the fighting had lasted nine hours thus far. The planes had made another approach on the southerly side of the mountain and had commenced firing upon positions 3 and 4 when ropes were cut down, and the mirrors exposed. The team members in positions 3 and 4 were called to get into the storage containers immediately, and they did. Joshua and Captain Roger flew their planes with the fireworks attached directly toward the incoming planes. This distracted them for several seconds. As the pilots looked back, the mirrors reflected the sun and the pilots were blinded because the sun was just at the right angle, making the pilots disoriented and both planes to crash into the side of the mountain just below the mirrors, and with a great explosion, the pieces of the plane, with fiery liquid from the fuel tanks, fell down upon the area around former positions 5b and the fake defensive area, taking out many fighters. The second plane's fiery ball landed in the area where the general and his command staff were standing, which took out the general and his entire command staff.

These two crashes shook our command center with their very noisy explosions. Rabbi Maskil became startled and dropped his staff, which he had been holding throughout the entire battle. This was the first time during the battles that he dropped his staff and quickly picked it up and held it high while praising God. He was very diligent because he feared that once he lowered his staff, the enemy might gain the advantage and someone might die as a result, as prophesied during the seventy days. The worship team was now singing "Go Tell It on the Mountain."

By now, all the fighters were now in the mountain pass, and the fighting was fierce, because the enemy had seen many of their friends killed. They were advancing, and our defense fighters in the water pipes and sewer pipes were picking them off as they reached within the fifty-foot mark away from the final defensive position. Lou had left his position with Gary and Moe and went down to assist Rick's team. He took the remaining ammunition and went into one of the sewer pipes that formed the V and commenced firing. Yet they kept coming and coming. While Lou was reloading, one of the enemy fighters spotted him and shot at him several times. The other defender was able to shoot the fighter, but not in time. Lou was killed, as prophesied, as a result of Rabbi Maskil dropping his staff. Jim and another service team member went to bring Lou's body to one of the trailers behind the final defensive position. Jim was very mad. Lou was his closest friend. He picked up Lou's gun and took his position fighting in the pipes. We kept on fighting, and our supplies were nearly exhausted. It was now six thirty in the evening. Rick called the command central that the fourth team member, Lou, was dead and that Jim took over his position. Jim told Rick, "That makes four, and I believe in God's promises: you do not need another paramedic, but you need a fighter."

Captain Roger's planes and drones were still flying around the area and verified to Colonel John that the last of the fighters had entered the mountain road pass between the two mountains. Colonel John gave the order to blow both levels of the mountain pass twelve seconds apart, as detailed in the plan. Rick's team fired the cannon one more time with the last of the cannonballs and coffee can containers of metal. The order was given for our defense teams to take shelter in the containers, and the colonel shouted the countdown, "Fire in the hole, five…four…three…two…one…blast off!" and the explosions were so great it even shook the mountain homes. Rick's team had just made it to the containers a split second before the first blast, and the force of the blast closed the door behind them. Then the second blast went off, and this blast was even more powerful than the first.

When our teams emerged from the containers to take our positions back on the ledge, all we saw initially was a huge gray cloud of dust everywhere, and when that cleared, we saw thirty feet of rock between the mountain passes. The rock flew up and covered up to twenty feet away from the final defensive position 5c. The remaining thousand or twelve hundred soldiers were buried beneath all that rock. The mountain pass looked like a quarry, with hundreds of thousands of tons of granite rock ready to be processed. The colonel called out for our troops to cease firing. The ladies had just finished singing "How Great Thou Art," and all was quiet. We looked out over the battlefield, and all we saw were bodies, body parts, rocks, and scorched earth. We felt relieved, but we did not rejoice in all those who had died. Instead, we felt great remorse in the poor, misled souls who could not be saved. They became puppets in the hands of

Satan to do his bidding. It was quiet for ten minutes. It took another ten minutes for the dust to settle. Rabbi Maskil and Pastor Dave shouted in unison, "Hallelujah, our God is alive, and He has won the victory! Hallelujah! You have won the victory for us, and You are the risen King of all!" Then Irene was heard shouting out, "Tetelestai!"

Rabbi Maskil then said, "That means 'it is finished' in Greek."

The worship team sang their final two songs on the list, which were "To God be the Glory" and "God Over All."

The final fight started at five thirty in the morning at the break of dawn, just at sunrise, and ended at seven forty in the evening, just before sunset. The enemy lost over six thousand more troops in this fight, and we lost four Vietnam vets. They did love the Lord, but did the two trust in their own wills and abilities or were disobedient as to their instructions? Why would one die because Rabbi dropped his staff? Were they great fighters but two enjoyed the kill more than the purpose of serving? Did their hearts become bitter with anger and retribution and they took their eyes away from the Lord, their God and Savior? These events were predicted by Irene and Estelle's word from the Lord on the seventieth day. We knew one repented, but did the others repent? We knew two gave their lives to protect others; would God accept the sacrifice of the other two, and would we see them at the golden gate? We knew our God is merciful, and we knew our God is righteous and just. We did know they accepted our Lord as their Savior. They may have been disobedient, but we have a merciful God.

The ladies and the chef prepared the meals, and they first served the refugees and the other women with their children under thirteen who were segregated in the middle school. We unlocked the high school after they were able to obtain a school bus and several vehicles and had the nearly eighty refugees transported to the refugee camp nearly eighty miles north of the village. Three of the refugees had been bus drivers in the past, so they were able to drive the school buses located at the school. We left the suspected infiltrators locked up at the jail and mental health facility. We radioed Captain Mark but spoke to his assistant that the eighty refugees were heading north in three school buses. We did not tell him the fighting was over. They brought the refugees to a checkpoint approximately twenty miles away, and our team member returned, telling the soldier nothing about the status of the fighting. We did not tell the refugees that the fighting was over, only that there was a lull in the fighting. We took the bodies of our fallen defenders to the town's mortuary for burial the following day.

We gathered at the command center to eat and praise the Lord for all He had done. After supper and service, we still stationed two defenders at stations 2, 3, 4, and 5c and sent replacements every four hours to relieve them. All was quiet during the night.

Ｗe awoke and gathered at the command center for praise and worship at sunrise on the seventh day. It was Sunday, and our service lasted for three hours. The loudspeakers were still blasting loudly, and the praise songs filled the valley to the south. We finished singing John Polce's song "Take My Hand," and the last verse and chorus words were thus:

Where would I be without Your love, who
would I be without Your mercy?
For all my days, Lord, I will praise You for
Your wonderful saving grace.
Your face is all that I see, your voice is all that I hear.
Come take My hand, I know the way.
Trust in Me and do not fear.

Just as we finished the last note, six armed ISISA fighters came into the room. We had thought they all were dead, but these six had stayed back in one of the armored personnel carriers. They were about to kill us when Irene, Estelle, Michelle, and Diane stepped forward and pointed at them, speaking in tongues. They pointed at the front three soldiers and, apparently, were saying in Arabic and in unison, "You will not kill anyone, you will drop your guns and surrender, and if you do not do this, Yahweh, the creator of all that has ever been created, will strike you dead." The soldiers laughed at them, and then the three soldiers in the front, at which the three ladies were pointing, suddenly fell down dead. The remaining three soldiers were in shock, and the ladies pointed to the three remaining soldiers and they quickly dropped their guns and placed their hands above their heads. The team members grabbed the guns and took the three fighters to the jail, locked them up, and fed them breakfast.

With that experience of having stray fighters up and about, Rick, Captain Gary, Pierre, Tom, Moe, Colonel John, and two-thirds of the other men went onto the battlefield to see if there were any more fighters left. They scoured the battlefield, armored vehicles, tanks, trucks, and the rocky road area for any survivors, and they did not find any. They picked up several weapons while Captain Roger, Joshua, and their team sent up five drones and planes to scour the mountainside and the area leading down to the lake villages. They only had a radius of three or four miles and could not go as far as the village below, which was about five or so miles away. They searched for six hours and could not locate any more fighters.

The guards at the jail asked the three survivors how many more soldiers were in the village south of us. At first, one of them said, "We have a hundred thousand more," in an immensely proud fashion. The guard told them that if they did not tell us the truth, we would have the four ladies come back and point their finger at them and they would surely die. They immediately told them that the general took all their fighting men and equipment to take the pass and only the women and young children remained in the village. They had killed all the remaining villagers before they left, except for the wives and children of the fighters. We asked about the one hundred sixty refugees sent to us and asked them how many of them were spies, and they responded about twelve men plus some women and children. This confirmed what we had discerned. We could tell that the three were not seasoned fighters. They appeared to be about eighteen years old.

Then the guards went to the middle school and brought the women and their children to the police station to be placed in separate jails in the basement level. The jails could house about thirty prisoners. About ten upstairs and twenty in the basement. When they entered, they saw the three fighters in the jails and asked where the others were. They responded that they did not know. They asked about the fighting, and they were told in Arabic that these evil Christian people were possessed with evil powers and that they had killed all the ten thousand fighters and they were the only three fighters alive. The women broke down in tears because their husbands and children were among the fighters. They were locked up in the lower jails with their children.

We felt confident there were no more fighters in the vicinity. First, we fed the prisoners and then we gathered for supper, and after supper, it was almost sunset, so we commenced praise and worship, which lasted over an hour.

Then several broke out into tongues as we praised Jehovah Nissi, the Lord of our victory, and we felt the presence of the Holy Spirit in the room. We were in deep worship when Irene, Michelle, Estelle, and Diane stepped forward. Alternating, they started to speak. "Well done, good and faithful servants. I have carved My name into your hearts, and you have done very well. As for this village and as for those who will travel here, and as for those who have a heart of stone, I have carved My name into the stone for all to see. The victory is Mine, says I, Yahweh, the creator of the universe, and now all will know that I, Yahweh, and My Son, Jesus, and our Spirit have claimed the victory over evil. Now they will know that I am God and you are My people. If they do not come back to Me, greater tragedies will befall before them when My Son and the heavenly host return.

"This battle and the eleven other similar battlegrounds will show the world that I am Lord. I am the protector of My remnant people, and My Son is the Way, the Truth, and the only Light unto the world. Evil will not overcome good. Darkness will not overcome the light. I have been tolerant for many generations. The remnant of My people who remain faithful will be greatly rewarded. The fake peace will occur soon, and My other faithful servants and those who have truly repented and have turned away from their evil will be taken up after the trumpet blows and with the shout to come to feast with me for seven of your earth years.

"This week, you have withstood much as I have strengthened you, but so that the world will know and give Me the victory, I will need to restore you back to where you were before the seventy days. This is not a punishment—your reward will be great. You all will soon be with Me, for I have prepared several mansions and a great feast in your honor in heaven upon your arrival. I have gathered all your loved ones that are with Me now, and they will be at the gate to greet you.

"The Army will return tomorrow and be in awe, especially when Captain Mark and his general sees what I have done through you. You will be with Me soon in paradise. Do not be afraid of coming to me. I have prepared a mansion for each of you, and My Son and the twelve, along with Abraham, David, Joshua, Elisha, Elijah, Moses, and the prophets, will greet you, My good and faithful servants. I eagerly await your arrival, and the banquet feast has been set. They have been proud of your obedience and the condition of your heart during your trials.

"Within the year, all of you will be with me. Gather every afternoon and write what you have seen and done and what you have experienced. I will leave one to tell the story of My mercy and My love, and I will call him last. Captain Mark will become a believer, and he will warn this nation to come back to their founding roots of My Son, Jesus. Just as I am merciful and forgiving, I am also just, and those who do not reverence My name, or My Son, will see My wrath and My justice when My Son returns with the host of warrior angels.

"I have given several of you nearly one year so that you may talk to your family, especially those family members who have strayed from My love, so you can remind them of their first love when they were children. I will start soon based upon those with the least faith to those with the greatest faith and trust. After this, they will know that I am God, loving, merciful, patient, yet just. If they do not repent, worse things will fall upon them, and I will give them three opportunities to turn from their evil ways and repent and reverence My Son and serve Me, just as you have. Again, all you good and faithful servants, the seventy times twelve, when you wake up in the morning, you will return to your former state, for the sake of My glory, not as a punishment. Enjoy the rest of the evening. Dance and be merry and be thankful for the twelve days you have had in which I restored the days of your youth. I love you and will see you soon."

We stayed in silence for another twenty minutes. Then Captain Roger, who had been crippled due to a stroke, and Pierre, who had been blind, shouted out and said, "What are we waiting for? It is time to party till midnight! Let the dancing begin!" So we feasted and partied until nearly midnight, and we all went home to rest, praising what the Lord had done.

I n the morning, we arose just before dawn and gathered at the
church. Those who were cripple and blind returned to their former state, those who had crutches, walkers, and canes needed
them to get around, and those who had aches and pains, they returned
also. No one complained because all were thankful for twelve days
of their youth. Twelve days of running, jumping, and enjoying life
again without suffering. Thankful for the six days the Lord put His
hedge of protection over our members. We praised the Lord and
worshipped for nearly two hours. After that, we cooked breakfast in
the church kitchen and served the prisoners first, then our members.
Late last night, Fran and Rene and the Bosnians, along with some of
their team members, went shopping at the food stores, knowing that
they would not be so nimble in the morning. We thanked them for
their foresight and for bringing it to the church kitchen.

After breakfast, we went back to the battlefield wondering what
we needed to do or, should I say, what we could do. As we sat behind
Rick's final defensive position, we saw nearly two dozen helicopters
come from the north. The first group flew by us and started to circle
the mountains; others went on to the next town. The last group of
helicopters landed five hundred feet away from us in the field and
the road. Just as they landed, thousands of troops and vehicles came
flooding in from the north road and stopped just before us.

Captain Mark and the general disembarked from one of the
helicopters and came walking over to us. Colonel John, Major Eric,
Captain Gary, Captain Roger (who we needed to roll over in the
wheelchair), and Lieutenant Bernie saluted the general, and Colonel
John said, "General, we stood our ground and did not let the enemy

through. We lost four fine soldiers who fought in Vietnam and served us bravely. Sixty-six of us survived and fought for every inch of ground, and we destroyed nearly eighty tanks, two hundred armored vehicles, four hundred trucks, and over ten thousand of the enemy fighters. We did not rejoice in killing so many, but we needed to stand our ground and prevent them from killing any more civilians or getting past us. We bought you the time you needed to regroup."

The general looked around and saw those using canes, walkers, crutches, and wheelchairs. He looked at us again, saluted back to the colonel, and said to Captain Mark, "What the hell is this? Is this the defense forces you were telling me about? Seventy old people who could hardly move defended this pass against so many young ISISA fighters?"

Colonel John immediately responded, "With all due respect, General, we had God on our side, and He gave us the strength to overcome these odds and gave us the defense plan, which we only executed on His behalf. Also, He even fought part of the battles all by Himself with the heavenly host as we watched in awe and wonder."

Just as the colonel finished, another officer who had just flown around the mountain, who had taken several pictures and viewed the carnage in the ravine and along the mountain, joined the group, and he spoke. "General, I have viewed the other side of the mountain, and you will not believe what I have seen. The ravine is filled with thousands of bodies and hundreds of pieces of equipment that have also been destroyed. Look at these pictures. We took them on our cell phones, about the carnage. This was an overwhelming victory for our forces."

The general looked at the pictures and then replied to the officer, "I would like to introduce to you the seventy brave soldiers who did this by defeating the ten thousand crack fighters you saw below." As he pointed to our church members, the officer said, "Where are they?" and the general pointed to us again and said, "This is Colonel John, Major Eric, Captain Gary, Lieutenant Bernie, and in the wheelchair is Captain Roger, who led those fighters to defeat the ten thousand ISISA fighters. Regretfully, they lost four soldiers who had fought in the Vietnam War."

The young officer said, "You're pulling my leg, aren't you?"

Then Captain Mark said, "Absolutely not. They are the same soldiers whom I helped for three days set up the defensive positions twelve days ago. I promised to be back on the fourth day to take over the fighting, but the general would not allow it because we were not ready to mobilize."

Colonel John said, "I regretfully have to tell you that all the neighboring villagers were killed by the fighters and the only remaining people in the village are the wives and children of the fighters, so please be cautious. In addition, we have three ISISA soldiers in the brig, and the wives and children of the dead fighters in a jail in the basement of the police station. I respectfully request that you take them off our hands. They are the only survivors of the more than ten thousand fighters Also, the women have transmitters in the back of their neck that communicated to the other fighters. You will need to remove them before your transport them back. I hope you brought along a surgeon to do this."

One of the helicopter pilots came walking over and saw Captain Roger and asked him, "What happened to you? Did you get shot?"

Captain Roger responded, "No. I just returned back to my old state when our mission was done."

"I don't understand!" replied the pilot. "You walked, ran, and flew my chopper for three days. You were fine. Are you saying you were crippled, then you were healed, and after this mission, you became crippled again?"

Captain Roger replied, "Exactly! I am very thankful that my God gave me the twelve days of my youth and let me fly once again."

The general chimed in and said, "How many more surprises are you going to tell me? This sounds like a science fiction movie or an old Alfred Hitchcock flick."

Captain Mark responded to the general, "You really do not know all the miracles that occurred here at this pass. God has the power to heal. I will ask these volunteers to tell you all about it after and during the debriefing." Captain Mark asked the general to remain with us so that we could debrief him and his command staff. The general ordered the construction battalion with their equipment to start clearing the pass and the roadway and for a division of troops to take control of the next village. He informed them of our warning. Captain Mark asked for a copy of the plans we used so he could show the general the creativeness of the defense.

Moe made copies of the plans and told him to tell the general that the creativeness was not from us but from the Creator of the universe and His name is Yahweh, as Captain Mark had promised to do so.

All that afternoon, we laid out what happened each day for the six days of battle for Captain Mark, the general, and his command staff, as well as the miracles God did for us. We told him about the six fighters and the three in the prison. We explained how God had rescued us involving the clouds, hail, and rain through the power of His Son's name. When Captain Mark asked about what the mirrors were for, we told them about the two planes the enemy sent and how they were blinded by the sun's reflection and how they crashed into the side of the mountain at the pass, killing the ISISA general along with his commanders. We told him about the several days of battle with their soldiers firing mortar rounds at us but the shells were either exploding in the air or were landing on their own soldiers and equipment. We explained that only a half-dozen rounds from tanks got through and went into the village, but we did not see what damage occurred due to our being busy in the heat of the battle. The general, Captain Mark, and their command staff were in awe, and not once did they laugh at us or mark us anymore.

That evening, the general, his officers, his command staff, and the twenty-four men who assisted us in setting up the defenses, and other selected soldiers, dined with us at the church hall as we retold the story of the seventy days, the three days of preparation, and the six days of fighting, and the two days after the fighting. The dinner lasted for hours. Instead of us serving the meals, the general ordered his chef and the enlisted men to serve us. We allowed them to do so, if they be allowed to sit and join us at the meal table and that Rabbi Maskil, Pastor Dave, and Father Jake be allowed to say the blessing and benediction before and after the meal, to which the general agreed.

Some of the officers were still in disbelief, but as a result of what they saw and the witness of Captain Mark and the men who assisted us in setting up for the battle, they confirmed all that we said and did. That Captain Roger was walking like a thirty-year-old and that Pierre could see better than most of us. They asked us if we were being punished because we returned to our former state of condition, and all said no. We needed to be healed to do the Lord's work. We were simply happy to have had twelve days of our youth restored, and God was so gracious and merciful to us. We even told them that we partied, danced, and praised the Lord the evening we knew we were going back to our previous conditions. We made the best of what we were given, and we thanked God for that short time. We also told them that we would be rejoicing knowing that within a year we would be given full restoration. The soldiers thought we were going to be restored back to health in a year when we were talking about returning to the Lord, because we were telling them with such a joyful and in peaceful tone.

The next morning, the soldiers started to clear the road, and they had brought in the Army Corps of Engineers and the construction battalion with heavy equipment to assist them. They also took much of the needed equipment from the quarry and local construction company. Before they did so, the general and Captain Mark ordered the helicopter pilots and members of Captain Mark's squad to take pictures of the area before they moved anything. They did and came back with hundreds of pictures, not only of the road, but also of the ravine. They could not believe the number of fighters that were killed. Once they made it through the pass, they started to just push the stones, rubble, bodies, and other debris over the cliff. They loaded up the items into dump trucks and dumped the debris and bodies from the pass over the cliff with the rest of the bodies, tanks, vehicles, and unusable equipment.

After they cleared off nearly a mile, the general, Captain Mark, Colonel John, Captain Gary, and Rabbi Maskil were offered a helicopter ride to tour the surrounding area. As they were flying back to the village from the ravine area, the general noticed a protrusion emanating from the south face of a rock or mountain. The general stated, "That is odd. Blasts do not cause that to happen!"

Rabbi Maskil looked and saw this strange writing אלהיבךֱההאהילך , and exclaimed, "Oh my god, *yod, he, vav, he* in Old Hebrew! These words read, 'I am Yahweh, your God.' This is our God of Israel and America, which is the only God, the God who saves. This is what God said He would do. He said He would carve His name into the hearts of His people, and so the villagers and visitors would see, he would carve his name into the stones because they have a heart of stone."

The general remarked, "Then you are telling me that your people did not do this?"

In unison, everyone replied, "No, this was done by the hand of God, as He said He would!"

The general's photographer took several pictures of the face of the hundred-foot stone wall that had been a result of that last southerly blast.

During that week, the Army moved into the neighboring villages and rounded up all the fighters' families into guarded concentration camps until they could figure out what to do with them. They also reported that the village of Zoar was significantly destroyed, burnt to the ground, except for a few stone or brick buildings. The town looked like a dump heap littered with trash and waste. They found thousands of bodies of the civilians in open graves, the men, women, and children of the villages. The enemy was so brutal to them. Many were butchered, the women raped and then killed. The men's and children's bodies were dismembered or just beheaded. They did find a few survivors who had hidden in the woods or pretended that ISISA forces were liberating them. They had horrific stories of survival.

It took the soldiers nearly a week to secure the fifty-mile area and clean out the roadways. The general enjoyed being with us for that extended period as the troops secured the area. While he was there, three of our church members passed away. The three who had no families or known relatives. When they were found, they all had a pleasant smile that portrayed a look of peace and joy on their face. We knew that this was going to happen during the year, but we did not think it would start this soon. The first three were also Vietnam vets who had been homeless, and now they were living in a mansion prepared by Jesus Himself.

One of the soldiers reported to the general that they found most of the bodies of the 156 soldiers who attempted to defend the village forty miles away. One of the soldiers was barely alive and severely wounded. His body was found beneath a pile of six other soldiers. The rest were all dead near the southern bridge coming into that village of Zoar. It looked like they fought to the death to the last man. They, too, did not retreat, but they were overwhelmed by too many forces with tanks. Their bodies were left there to rot by the enemy. The sole survivor was able to talk about their bravery.

We continued to meet at sunrise, and again at sunset, to thank the Lord and praise Him for reviving this great nation. Many of the soldiers, especially those who helped in the setup of the defenses, came to our worship service, and the church was filled.

They brought the bodies of the 155 soldiers, and we had sectioned off an area in our church cemetery to honor those who fought and died in service of their country. We placed our seven members who died adjacent to these soldiers' graves. Even our members were granted military honors and funerals. Our members as well as the 155 soldiers had a white cross with the simple words inscribed thereon: "We stood our ground so others may live." Captain Mark said he would keep six of his men and a lieutenant behind to do likewise for one year.

At each of the funeral services, either Pastor Dave or Rabbi Maskil conducted the service, and the worship team always sang one song at the grave site, which was "I Will Stand My Ground, Where Hope Can Be Found."

The general allowed the villagers to return home and ordered his remaining men to escort the refugees back to Bethel and the other neighboring towns north of the pass.

Ten days later, the villagers returned in their campers, trucks, and vehicles. They expected to see their homes and village destroyed—the Army never told them about what they had seen in Bethel. The first group to arrive was composed of the mayor, the selectmen, and the ten who ran away before the fighting started. Much to their surprise, most of the town was intact, except for the items we dismantled in the defense of the town. There were only six homes that had been hit and destroyed by the tank fire. Ironically, they were the homes of Billy the bully, the mayor, and four of the five councilmen. We were sure they would blame us for that, said Rabbi Maskil.

Captain Mark and a member of his squad greeted them. Captain Mark had copies of the pictures taken prior to the cleanup and had them set up in the high school auditorium as a display. They also took pictures of the sixty-six who were alive when they returned and obtained pictures of the four who had died defending the village. Just above the pictures of the seventy was a caption entitled, "The God Squad, under the command of Yahweh and His Son, Yeshua, support by the Holy Spirit and their heavenly host air force." Some listed, "Mission: Operation Stand Your Ground," with the caption beneath the picture stating, "Trust without borders, courage like no other." We loved it. It was so true.

The picture showed Colonel John, Major Eric, Captain Gary, and in the center, Captain Roger in his wheelchair. The rest of the men surrounded them, with their wives next to them. Those that needed walkers or crutches were seated with their walker or crutch in front of them. Those with canes were holding them up and forming a V for victory.

After the rest of the villagers returned to their homes, the general requested (more like ordered) the villagers to come to the high school that evening for debriefing. Most of the villagers showed up, except the ten who had pretended to stay and fight did not go. They had told many people when they were at the refugee camp how brave they were and how they would kick butt with the enemy. Now they could not face the people they bragged to, because they were not among the defenders. They were too embarrassed to show their faces.

At first, our church group did not know that a town meeting had been called, because we were at the church, praising and worshipping God. Then the general and Captain Mark asked us to join them in a debriefing session at the high school. When we entered through the rear door, the general took us to the stage area and had us sit down facing him, with the curtain being closed. We didn't hear some noises because of the loud military music playing in the background, and we were unaware that they had gathered the whole town. The general had Captain Roger, Colonel John, Major Eric, Lieutenant Bernie, and Captain Gary in the center, with the rest of us surrounding them, just as in the picture they had previously taken. The Army had blown up pictures of the four who died in the battle, plus the three who had died during the past week, and they were on display on the stage. When the general pulled the curtain, we were confused, as the townsfolk stood up and applauded. We did not want the glory.

The mayor and the lead selectman walked onto the stage to give a speech, but Captain Mark stopped them and asked them to get off the stage. He told them, "This is not a time for politics." After a few exchanges of words, the soldiers who had assisted us in the three days of preparation stood up and removed the officials, who became indignant, and the officials walked out of the hall.

The townsfolk were under the impression that the soldiers had retaken the town, but the general started off by saying, "While we were regrouping up north, seventy people from this town defended it, and that is why all of you have a home to go back to. These are the seventy people who stayed, fought, and some died so you may live. If they had not done so, we would not have had the time to regroup. You would not have a home to go back to. I would ask them to stand and take a bow, but they will not, and some cannot.

"We have taken pictures of the battlefield as it was when we arrived. These seventy fended off over ten thousand crack ISISA fighters with tanks, armored vehicles, and trucks for one week and not only defended this pass but destroyed them also. All ten thousand, except for three prisoners, have been killed. I ask the soldiers standing next to the walls to remove the coverings so that the people of this town, the photographers, and the newsmen can see what they did. The title of this fight will now be known as 'Operation: Stand Your Ground,' and these brave fighters will be known as the God Squad under the command of Yahweh and His Son, Jesus, with the support of the Holy Spirit and heavenly host air force. For those who do not believe in God, you ought to now think twice. God, with the help of these senior citizens, defended this village. When you look at these pictures, know that God gave them a defense plan and they executed that plan with precision and passion. I wish all my soldiers had the faith, the trust, the courage, and the discipline these seventy displayed. Look at these pictures, and if you do not come away in awe of what was accomplished here, then you are just a bunch of ungrateful, miserable people. I also want you to look at the last picture here at the stage. We have put this on the screen. It is the mountain wall facing the south, where the defenders fought their last battle. I want you to know that God protected them and the victory was God's."

The general went on to say, "The seventy looked at the picture and exclaimed to me what God had told them on the morning of the last battle. To cut it short, they said God told them He would write His name in their hearts but also, since the town had a heart of stone, He would write His name in the stone. Look carefully at the picture. Look at this outline. These words are in Hebrew, and the words say, 'I AM WHO I AM [Yahweh], the only God.' So for those who do not believe, please come and explain how this got there and how seventy senior citizens can destroy ten thousand crack fighters."

The general asked if anyone of us wanted to say anything, and Rabbi Maskil was first to get up and go to the podium. He said, "The general is correct. The words are in Hebrew, and God said He would write His name on this town, just as He did in Jerusalem. Yahweh is His name, and His Son's name is Jesus. The seventy church members are from different denominations, such as Catholic, Protestants, former Muslims who believe Jesus as the Messiah and Jews who also believe, not only in Yahweh, the Father, but in His only begotten Son and our Lord and Savior, Jesus Christ, whom we denied for two thousand years. Hear, O America, the Lord your God is one!"

As the rabbi was concluding, both Pastor Dave and Father Jake also arose and stood next to Rabbi Maskil. Pastor Dave said, "This country was founded on the Judeo-Christian principles of believing in the God of Abraham, Isaac, and Jacob. We have strayed so far from Him in the past fifty years. God is going to start a revival, and it will begin here. He wants America to return to Him. This village is named Bethel, which means in Hebrew 'house of God.' We are so loved by Him that He even carved His name in the mountain of our village as a welcome sign to all who come here. He spared your lives and your homes. They will forget about us because we are not important. We are just servants of God who simply listened, obeyed, and trusted Him by doing His will to execute His plan. He is the potter, and we are the clay. The carving of His name in the mountain by His hand will last forever, until His Son, Jesus, comes again in Jerusalem."

Pastor Dave said, "Our church believes in being more than a follower of Jesus, but we strive to be a disciple. It is much harder to be a disciple than a follower. To be Christlike takes you from the crowd into His inner circle. We need to embrace the cross and leave the world behind."

Anyone wishing for us to pray with them, please come to the stage area and our prayer teams will pray with you, and you, too, can accept the Lord, our Savior, so Jesus can carve His name in your hearts as well."

Just then, Billy, that extreme liberal and verbose village bully, who had given Captain Mark trouble before, the same one who was shot by his soldier in the leg and foot, came forward on his crutches and started mouthing off again by saying, "Don't give us that poppy-cock bull. There is no God—we are all gods!"

At that, Irene, Michelle, Estelle, and Diane came forward in unison on the stage and pointed directly at him, and they said, "You truly do not believe what you said."

Arrogantly he responded, "Okay, if there is a God, let Him strike me dead right now if I am wrong."

The four ladies pointed to the heaven and then pointed back to him again and said in unison, "Jesus, the Lord of righteousness and justice, grant him his request so all will know that You exist and defended this village." Immediately, he fell to the ground dead. After a few minutes of awe and silence as to what just happened, there was a mad rush to the stage area to be prayed with and to accept Jesus as Lord and Savior. All were silent, and as they awaited their turn to go to the stage, others started to go around the auditorium, looking at the pictures. They saw all the dead bodies and destroyed equipment in the ravine. They saw the rubble and road filled with tons of stone and more bodies and destroyed equipment. They saw the writing on the mountain in Hebrew, with its interpretation in the caption beneath the picture.

They saw the pictures of those old people in wheelchairs, walkers, and canes who defended the pass. They saw the statements made by the Army general and Captain Mark verifying all that happened to be true, and the pictures of the twenty-four soldiers and four helicopter pilots who assisted in the preparation. The only pictures not shown were pictures of the ten who assisted in the preparation but left before the battles. Somehow, they were never in any picture that the captain's men took. Finally, they saw a picture of the dated June 29, 2028, detailed plans for each defensive position and a listing of what was to be utilized in the defense of each position, as drafted by the Lord. In addition, they saw the seventy days of prophecies written weeks before the occurrence of the attacks. Revival started in the town that night, and most of the villagers and all the soldiers in Captain Mark's company received the Lord that night, even Billy's family. It soon spread to neighboring villages and then throughout the region.

We were there until sunrise, praising the Lord. The church was now too small for the service, and so now we met at the high school auditorium on Sundays. No one ever raised the issue of the separation of church and state again. In addition, they passed new laws prohibiting the government (federal, state, and local) from interfering with Judeo-Christian worship services and practices and allowed worship services in public facilities. The government now realized that all would have been lost if God had not intervened to protected America.

The townsfolk were in total awe of what happened during the nearly thirty days they were gone. The media reported the events, and they made TV specials about the events that occurred in our village. During the special television productions, the media also reported on eleven other similar events throughout the country. When they compared the plans of the defense, they all involved mountain passes and they were all so similar. Each of the other eleven dramatic defenses were defended by seventy elders who were all believers. At every one of the other eleven locations, carved by the hand of God into the mountain was God's name, Yahweh. To be exact, the actual subscription was, "Yahweh was with us." No one could deny that God's hand was upon the other eleven groups of seventy. They, too, were all miraculously healed before the period of preparation, and they were returned to their former state three days after the battle. They, too, were of mixed Christian denominations and all had at least one rabbi believer among them. The names of the other villages they defended all had Hebrew names or origins. The names of the eleven village passes defended by God were Kedesh, Shiloh, Gilgal, Tyre, Bethlehem, Hormah, Joppa, Jazer, Golan, Nebo, and Jarmuth. After looking at a map of old Israel when the twelve tribes took possession of the land, which God promised, Father Jake and Rabbi Maskil had previously noted that these were the names of twelve villages representing the twelve divisions of land among the twelve Jewish tribes.

We also found out that during the fighting in America and in Europe, no one attacked Jerusalem in Israel. Instead, the Israelites came to assist the Americans to defeat caliphates in America and

England. The Canadians in the north and Mexicans in the south also assisted by sending armies and air force personnel and planes.

Every day since the townsfolk returned, we gathered at noon to record all that occurred during the seventy days, the three days of preparation, and the six days of battle. Each of the defensive position commanders and command central location appointed the seven scribes to write what you have just read in this manuscript. We needed to talk about the love and mercies God displayed during the twelve days of protection and how He protected us while we executed His work.

There were numerous things found at the battle site that sent shivers down our spine when we first noticed them. The first was about the crosses at the three main areas of defense. Defensive positions 3, 4, and 5 all had a large thirty-five-foot cross for each to keep their focus upon when they started to doubt. Despite the hundreds of thousands of bullets flying toward our troops and positions, each of the crosses only had five puncture marks in the exact same places. Each of the puncture marks was at the location of where Jesus's five wounds on His hands, feet, and side were punctured.

The second remarkable event was the three large American flags at the same locations had exactly fifty puncture marks in the middle of each of the stars. There were no bullets on any of the stripes at all. Was God trying to tell us something?

During the eleven months after the final battle, we gathered statements by all the members to see how God worked in their lives before and during the battles. Everyone had moments that defined them and revealed their moments of faith, trust, and inspiration. The members did not define their moment of courage and trust but that of the other members and how they had inspired them and how they had restored their courage. They revealed the dramatic moments when someone either saved them or when they received a dramatic moment of encouragement and strength given to them by the Lord through other members. It was not only the fighters that were heroes, but there were more instances of thanksgiving for the service team and worship team. The songs of encouragement came at the exact right time, when many of our defense teams felt like giving up, felt overwhelmed, tired, afraid, or became discouraged. The service team and medics risked their lives to run through a barrage of bullets and rockets to bring supplies and ammunition to the frontline fighters. While others were retreating to the next defensive position, it was the medics that pushed forward to drag the bodies of our fallen soldiers to safety, just as Rick had previously done in the first instance. They were not going to let the enemy desecrate God's holy temple of a righteous person. After Rick's Marine slogan "No man left behind," this became the rule of the medics. We saw bullet holes through their uniforms and hats, but not one bullet wounded the medics and service team members. Their courage encouraged all of us. Their fearlessness emboldened all of us. The songs planned by the Lord were structured not only to aggravate the enemy but to also encourage the defenders.

It has been nearly eleven months since the last battle. The groups that died first were the single members, and then members who were widows and did not have a child in the village, and lastly, those who were married with children. The married members died together during their sleep with their children. Apparently, this way no one would grieve for a lost spouse or child. As of the last of the writings, of the those who defended the town, there are only eleven of us left; they are Moe and Irene, Rick and Diane, Captain Gary and Michelle, Joshua, Hailey, Tom and Monique, and me, Rabbi Maskil. It could be it was to enable all our children and grandchildren to come to the Lord. Michelle and Monique were Moe and Irene's daughters who had ten grandchildren and several great-grandchildren. Pastor Dave and his wife just went to meet the Lord last night. Father Jake was one of the first to go after the homeless vets.

Why were we the last to go? As the old Beatles song goes, "I don't know, I don't know." It could be that they were the first to step out in faith. We will all find out within the next month.

Within the two weeks before the completion of the year, Moe, Irene, Michelle, Gary, Hailey, Josh, Tom, and Monique died within minutes of one another, and then a week later, Rick and Diane passed away. Looking back, I noticed that the couples and families died together. The Lord is good, and all is well with my soul. Because they died as families at the same time, this showed it was a gracious act by God.

I leave a prophetic word to the new believers, a word from Gabriel, who was accompanied by Michael, who had been detained a second time by the prince of Persia. His message is as follows: "To the remnant of my faithful remnant, tell the new faithful to be aware of the 'Oth,' because now is the 'Moed of Yum Hakeseh,' and the mystery of the hidden week will soon be upon you, and then the great hidden day, the end of the last day. Jacob's trouble, as told by Daniel, my faithful servant, is about to begin. The frequency of the birth pains has increased, and the signs in the heavens have been given to you. Part of the heavens will fall upon you soon. The trumpet will sound soon because the watchmen have their shofars on their lips. The wedding feast is prepared, and the Lord is coming for His bride. The beast and the false prophet are about to assume their roles. They know their time is short. I have gathered the twelve thousand from each of the twelve tribes of Israel, and their work and mission are about to begin. The anointed of Zadok have been chosen, the holy of holies of Aaron, who have not abandoned me and have stayed close to the teachings of the righteous son of Shem, have been anointed. Isaiah and Enoch will arrive in the middle of the set time, and they will be in Jerusalem as 'Ha-ish omed,' and those left behind after I have summoned the righteous out of their graves and I catch up the rest of my faithful servants, they will need to know the truth and 'Amad' for My Word. My angels have been assembled, and the white horses have been mounted. The seven angels have their shofars, and when all have heard the blast of that last mighty trumpet, the King of Kings and Lord of Lords will move forth to Jerusalem. The time of difficulty will be the time to sow, and the Lord will give power and might to those who have faith and trust in the Word. God is the same God that delivered Joseph, David, Paul, and Peter. Stay in the Word and not in the crisis. Your confidence in the Lord will be greater than the setbacks or the trials."

The writing of these events was gathered by Moe, Pastor Dave, Rick, George, and one member from each defensive position, then forwarded to me to assemble and to finalize the message of Yahweh's mercy, love, and grace. Why was I chosen to be one of the last? Well, someone had to finish writing the manuscript. Some may take this as fiction, some may take it as just another attempt to revive a hopefully dead religious belief, but believers will know and believe this to be prophetic. Time will tell.

I needed to call Captain Mark, and I did. He was to carry this manuscript to the designated place. Since he was the first to believe from the military, and was now a true believer; I trusted in the Lord, who indicated that he was to deliver the manuscript to the proper person.

The world must know that God is to be given the credit for defending this town. We were only the supporting participants of this wondrous miracle and awe of the Lord.

I am now overpowered with peace and joy. The Lord, my God, is filling me with His love. My last words to the remnant are, "Come, Lord Jesus. Your servant is ready."

Sincerely yours in Christ Jesus,
Rabbi I. Ariel Maskil

added by Captain Mark

Rabbi Maskil had called me a week earlier and asked me to please come see him before the one-year anniversary of the final battle. It was Saturday, and I had to report to my old command center just fifty miles north of the town, so I thought I would spend Saturday and Sunday with the rabbi. While driving back to the town from the south, I noticed another different, man-made inscription carved into the mountain on the south wall of the western mountain, being the south side of Moe's and Irene's home. The inscription read, "1 Cor. 14:24–25." I thought this might be a passage from 1 Corinthians. I started to go back to church to read the Bible that Rabbi had given me last year.

I drove up to the church around noon and went in looking for the rabbi and found him in the pastor's office, slumped over the desk. Just as I entered the room, the song playing on his radio by K-Love was "I'm Coming Home." Next to him was the manuscript, the Torah, and the Holy Bible. I felt the rabbi's pulse, but his body was cold and there was no pulse. I called the police chief, and it took him ten minutes to come to the church. While I was waiting, I looked up 1 Corinthians and went to verses 24 and 25, and it stated, "But if all prophesy, and an unbeliever or an uninformed person comes in, he is convinced by all, he is convicted by all. And thus, the secrets of his heart are revealed; he will worship God and report that God is truly among you."

As I looked at marked passages in the rabbi's Bible, I noticed several passages about the seventy disciples Jesus sent out two by two into the world to perform miracles and bring the good news. And the passage about the twelve disciples in the upper room and the eleven disciples He first appeared to after His resurrection from the dead when doubting Thomas was present.

I said to myself, "Wow, now I know why God selected eleven other locations, one location for each of the disciples, and why He selected seventy for each location, one village for each of the twelve tribes." As my mind became open to many revelations about the meanings and the significance of the events, the numbers, the trust, and the courage of the believers, it was like a big ten-thousand-piece puzzle coming together at once. The names of the villages being defended were the twelve regions after Joshua took possession of the land in Israel. Someone also had shown me a picture of the city of Jerusalem from a satellite looking down on the city from twenty thousand feet. Yahweh's name, just like the name carved into the mountains, was also carved in the street patterns within the old portion of the city of Jerusalem. Yahweh leaves His mark on what He claims as His.

It is true that "God so loved the world that He gave His only Son and He also gave us twelve sets of seventy believers willing to die in His service to prove to us that He still loves us today and until His Son returns."

I truly believe that, according to Revelations, the final great battle will be in Israel and will be known as the battle of Armageddon, when the Son of Yahweh returns with His heavenly host. Jesus, who will stand on Mount Moriah and defend His holy city of Jerusalem, will defeat the two hundred million troops descending upon His holy city, and as Mr. Wonderful often said, "They will be crushed like the cockroaches they are." The ten thousand who descended upon this town were crushed by the hand of God and thrown into a lake of fire.

Operation: Stand Your Ground was nothing less than a miracle of biblical proportions. The carving into the mountain walls after the explosions is totally unexplainable and not caused by man. The awe and wonder shown to the world at Bethel and the eleven other locations during the same six days cannot be refuted or denied. Yahweh's name left on the twelve mountains stands as the proof that God defended all the passes, and He left His mark caved in stone for generations to see, because each of the seventy defenders at each location had His name carved within their hearts. Pastor Dave told me, "Faith is trusting in God though the situation does not seem right or possible."

As I picked up the manuscript, the Torah, and the Bible, I noticed a scripture was written on a sheet of paper, which listed Malachi 4:1–6. This was the last prophet and the last chapter of the Old Testament. I wonder what significance this means.

This final battle is one battle I hope to be part of, and I believe this will occur in Jerusalem, when the Yahweh sends His Son to defend the Lord's city and conquer evil once and for all. I envy those who will be there to witness God's awe and majesty.

Signed,

Captain Mark

Captain Mark, US Army

CPSIA information can be obtained
at www.ICGtesting.com
Printed in the USA
BVHW022150140621
609612BV00017B/573